The End
of Fossil Energy

and
A Plan for Sustainability

M^cINTIRE
·PUBLISHING·

The publisher gives permission for any part of this publication to be reproduced with appropriate reference and not for profit and/or resale.

ISBN 0-9743404-0-5

The editors for this book were Don McLean and Debbie Howe. The production supervisor was Ginny Howe. It was set in Janson by McIntire Publishing.

Printed and bound by Network Printers, Milwaukee, WI.

For more information please contact the author at: Howe Engineering Company, P.O. Box 2038, Norway, ME 04268 or McIntire Publishing Services through their website at: www.mcintirepublishing.com

The End
of Fossil Energy

and
A Plan for Sustainability

by John Howe

5 - 14-04

MᶜINTIRE
·PUBLISHING·

Dedication

To my children and all the children of the world...
they will need all the resources we can conserve.

Dedication

Contents

Acknowledgments

I would like to directly acknowledge the leadership of Dr. Colin Campbell, the founder of the Association for the Study of Peak Oil and Gas (ASPO). You can download a wonderful picture of this distinguished Irish gentleman as well as the following quotation from the ASPO website, www.peakoil.net.com:

> *"Understanding depletion is simple. Think of an Irish pub. The glass starts full and ends empty. There are only so many more drinks to closing time. It's the same with oil. We must find the bar before we can drink what's in it."*

If the world survives the looming energy crisis, it will largely be because of this one man's efforts.

*   *   *

On a personal level, three people have been indispensable during the preparation of this book:

Don McLean, D.V.M., a lifelong, alternative lifestyle and renewable energy enthusiast who practices what he preaches. Don has been a hands-on mentor for all things relating to energy as well as number one critic for my English composition.

Ginny Howe, my daughter, is a career graphic artist and publisher. Her knowledge allowed me to transform my manuscript into a printed book.

Debbie Howe, my loving wife, patient sounding board, and keyboard link to the outside world.

Preface

I'm sitting in a rural New England farmhouse in February 2003 trying to start this project for the fifth time in the last 10 years. The setting could not be more ideal in my comfortable, senior years as a retired engineer, farmer, part time historian, and sometimes skeptic. Yet, something seems terribly wrong. It's a cold winter day, and in the last few minutes the back-up oil burner has switched on to smooth out the heat from our woodstoves. Now, silence is disturbed again by the school bus delivering the neighbor's children. A huge logging truck just trundled down the road with wood destined for who knows where; it varies, pulp for one of the paper mills, saw logs for Japan, or maybe just biomass for chipping and electrical cogeneration. A skidder is still roaring into the late afternoon, and a jet has left the east coast swinging west overhead. Fortunately, the snowplow is only sanding today, and our driveway is clear thanks to a gallon of gas in our 50-year old John Deere tractor.

The sound of energy intrudes, as does the TV reporting the latest on the pending war in Iraq (which just happens to have over 100 billion barrels of conventional oil reserves, the second largest in the world after Saudi Arabia). The war news is frequently interrupted by ads for things we must have, like 4 x 4 pick up trucks and snowmobiles.

Our president mentioned hydrogen fuel in his State of the Union address the other night. It's hard for me, as an engineer, farmer, and manufacturer of bicycle powered generators, to imagine a hydrogen-powered school bus, skidder, snowplow, tractor, jet plane, etc. I'm sure he means well, but wonder if he understands the language of BTU's, watts, kilowatt hours, and calories as well as the details of non-fossil energy sources like solar, nuclear, wind, geothermal, bio, and hydro.

There is a hard-to-resist pressure to consume and throw away, because our fast paced materialistic lifestyle is built on a foundation of very low cost fuel. From consumer goods shipped from China to a supermarket full of food or a tank of gasoline, energy is an integral part of our lives. Yet, we know intuitively, and many experts are telling us, this present epoch cannot last much longer. There are many sources of energy to do our work (other than food which fuels our muscles). The fossil fuels are inexpensive and supply 86% of our needs, but they exist in limited quantities. Renewable energy resources, like solar and wind, will last forever but presently contribute only a tiny part of our total consumption.

All the things I've mentioned are small pieces of a huge puzzle. The picture becomes much clearer after years of collecting and studying the pieces. The emerging composite is so ominous and frightening that I feel compelled to speak out. I must try to reach as many people as possible while there is still time to act and there are remaining resources to facilitate change. This is a compelling story that concerns everyone and needs to be told. There are many similar voices with more credentials and better words than mine, but they are on the web or in obscure, technical, and expensive books. One thing I will try to do differently is to condense the energy story into one small book, which will summarize and bring to date the subject in a manageable form. I will self-publish the first three thousand copies for free distribution and attempt to reach as many as possible with the facts. Please read on and get involved as an informed citizen demanding answers, action, and who will vote for equally concerned leaders to get us moving in the right direction.

The astonishing communication power of the World Wide Web is unique to our age. Electronic information may be a key source for quickly providing facts, resources, and opportunities for public involvement. If you have any doubts concerning the coming crisis, I suggest you first turn to Chapter 3 which lists an ever-growing number of pertinent websites and a ground swell of concern about the demise of fossil fuels. Unfortunately, only a fraction of the public uses the web. Too many rely on simplistic TV which does not focus on scary projections, especially those that might offend advertisers or consumer market segments.

By the spring of 2004, this energy book will be published. The public has to become involved and time is of the essence. On August 14, 2003, a series of obscure "natural" (does this mean non-terrorist?) events shut down the electricity in the eastern one third of the United States from New York City to Cleveland to Canada. Officials scrambled to find what went wrong and how to prevent it from reoccurring. This event serves to show how important just the electrical component of energy is in our complex society, yet most of the American public is still unaware of the facts showing the 100-year epoch of low cost energy is clearly entering its twilight period. This will surely lead us to a much different future. More power plants and transmission lines are not the solution without fuel to feed them. Honest energy legislation should first focus on long term availability of basic fuel sources.

Every citizen of the modern world should know the story of energy because everyone is a participant. The outcome will depend on all of us working together. Cataclysmic times are at our doorstep. We, our children, and our grandchildren cannot expect to continue the energy intoxication of the 20th century.

Post Preface

The epilogue to the story of fossil energy cannot be written for another fifty years. By then I would be 120 years old so I probably won't be here. At the present time, depletion of oil, natural gas, and coal seem to be a silent topic, at least in the USA. Could this be intentional because the subject is so horrific or just denial? Obscure websites or offhand mention in the media relegates energy to the status of dubious science or conspiracy theories. For example, the Jan 22, 2004 issue of *The New York Times* discusses the January 9th announcement by Shell that they are drastically reducing their oil proven reserve estimate by 3.9 billion barrels. Instead of mentioning the possibility of world depletion, the article focuses on investor "significant concern and in some quarters, outrage" against management and the form of corporate structure.

The status quo is extremely discouraging considering the small time frame we have for the changes we must make. The next several years will show if we are up to the task.

chapter 1

Energy Crisis Overview

We are on a collision course with disaster. In the last four generations (100 years), we have built a very tall house of cards and enjoyed a party provided by plentiful, lowcost fossil fuel. We've developed the technology to convert plentiful energy into an easy lifestyle. This has been going on just long enough that few in the developed nations remember what life was like before this luxury. It took hundreds of millions of years for the earth to accumulate various forms and small pockets of concentrated fuel. Now, we are using it at such a prodigious rate that at least the liquid and gaseous components will become scarce in the next decade. The age of stored fossil fuel energy will have lasted, in total, only about 200 years. A similar life-altering asteroid might impact the earth every few hundred million years. Our manmade crisis is at our doorstep now. Rather than denying this, leaving our survival to others, or just giving up, read on. There may be a way to achieve a sustainable civilization. It is up to us as intelligent individuals acting in concert to identify and follow that path. We are the problem. We are the only hope for the solution. Time is critical. Every moment wasted means less chance for survival.

For thousands of generations our ancestors subsisted in a delicate, harsh balance with the environment. Like all organisms

1

our bodies have the ability to produce at least enough energy to procure food (fuel) which, in turn, provides our personal energy along with a little left over to fight with competitors for resources or to procreate and survive lean times. In good years, human population increased because the population of any species reflects the abundance of the environment. As soon as the resources dwindled, either because of resource depletion or climate change, the population declined. This forced the population to remain stable for tens of thousands of years.

Since the rapid advance of technology in the last century, which enabled us to utilize previously stored highly concentrated energy, world population has exploded at an exponential rate from one billion people to six billion.

Any dynamic increase like population growth or resource consumption cannot last. The greater the growth or movement in one direction, the more severe will be the ultimate correction. What goes up must come down.

Some changes are imperceptible in our human time frame. It takes recorded history, archeological research, and science to accurately understand the past, assess the facts, and predict the future. To deny these natural and scientific observations will be our demise.

Less intelligent species can be forgiven for not seeing or reacting to the external forces which control population and resource consumption. Humans, on the other hand, are gifted with magnificent brainpower and the ability to learn from the past and plan for the future. Yet, we are blind if we don't use our extreme intelligence to anticipate and hopefully cushion our impending collision with the coming energy and closely related population crises.

There are many voices in the wilderness warning of the impending crash, but for all practical purposes nothing is happening. We are just shrinking the time frame to our demise. Later in this book I discuss further the movement of environmentalism. Why we don't want to hear or act on these messages is varied.

One author, Peter Seidel, in his book *Invisible Walls*[1] has directly addressed this subject. Time is rapidly running out. We will soon lose any opportunity to act appropriately while we do nothing but let short-term interests determine our path.

If we lose the advanced technology we are presently enjoying, no future civilization will ever again be able to achieve a similar level of freedom from human labor. The fossil fuels and their support of our lifestyle will be forever lost.

The necessary downsizing of consumption will require many changes. These need to be understood and made by all, not just a few. The only hope for survival on our life raft is for leadership and peer pressure to insure that everyone shares the commitment and a few don't rob the provisions. Fortunately, much of the industrialized world is ruled by democracies with elected leaders who should answer to informed constituents and not to inanimate corporate structures concerned primarily with short term profits regardless of the impact on natural resources.

In the 2004 critical election year we in the U.S. must support candidates most concerned with the immediate impact of energy on the survival of humankind.

Our present complacency is encouraged by a mix of the following (not essentially in order):

• **The crisis is not urgent. Leave it to future generations.** Wrong! The crisis is here now. In the next 10 years, major changes will begin to occur. The direction of these changes depends on us. Our children will be left with nothing but scraps if we don't act now. The sooner we start to reduce our fossil fuel consumption, the more hope we have. We are stealing the future from everyone.

3

- **Religion and prayer will save us.** Wrong! God is sending us a message now. We should heed it well. The free energy party is man-made including all the luxuries we take for granted: cheap and plentiful food, plush and easy transportation, warm houses, and hot baths. We cannot even return to the harsh existence of the Middle Ages. There are too many people now, and in the industrialized world, we have lost our subsistence skills. If heaven and afterlife are the salvation for some, we are not leaving enough finite resources for our earthly descendants.

  The religious community may in fact be a ray of hope in its recognition of the energy crisis and call to action as stewards of the earth. There is a groundswell of activity by Christians, Muslims, and Jews joining with other beliefs in a common concern for environmentalism and the subject of finite fuel sources. Prompt dissemination of the energy crisis message may be facilitated through religious networks.

- **The scientists will save us.** Wrong! After scientists taught us how to use essentially free, previously stored, fossil energy, they are now telling us we are running out. Unfortunately, the public is not hearing this message, possibly because it is in complex books and technical language. An exception is the excellent book, *Hubbert's Peak*.[2] This recent book explains in clear, undeniable detail the history and consumption of petroleum as our most important fossil fuel. It makes little difference if we have 20 or 40 years left. The truth is, we can't go on this way. The more we have left and the sooner we start to conserve, the better our chance for survival.

  Chapter 2 is an attempt to simplify the science of energy. In Chapter 3 I will introduce the necessary numbers required for an understanding of our past and present energy usage. Comprehensive data for world oil production are shown in Appendix 5. To eliminate confusion, all numbers will be converted to equivalent units of billions of barrels of oil (EBBO). In Chapter 4, I envision a low energy, future model of a modern society. Chapter 5 defines a Five Percent Plan to reduce energy usage to a sustainable future level.

One other important point to keep in mind is that any possibility for a significant, high technology future requires the springboard of a functioning, energy intensive society such as we have today. The infrastructure and investment required for controlled nuclear fusion or other energy related breakthroughs are not going to come out of the ashes of anarchy or a failed civilization.

- **There is a strong environmental movement growing in the world today.** Unfortunately, the messages are soft, sometimes misdirected to other priorities and may lead to false complacency. Other weaknesses of well-meaning, nonprofit organizations are:

1. They churn around and around preaching to the choir, their own members. With memberships of up to a million, each is still less than one percent of the U.S. population. They are not reaching enough of the masses to be effective. Glossy periodicals and tiny environmental actions delude the public into thinking there is progress. Wrong! We are losing ground, especially with leadership (right or left) concerned with re-election based on optimism, near term gratification, and, where deemed necessary, military intervention to maintain energy resource flow with little or no planning for future supplies and resources.

2. Even the closely related subject of climate change is not making an impact since the time frame is measured in hundreds of years not decades. Not many people care. The public doesn't feel an urgent crisis. They may think global warming would require less energy for heating (or plowing snow) and be a good thing. Global warming will become a more serious problem after we run short of oil and natural gas, and obtain more and more of our energy from dirty fossil fuels like high sulfur coal and difficult to extract sources like tar sands and shale oil. By that time, in a few years, our civilization will already be in serious trouble if we do not address the immediate problem of

5

dwindling cleaner fuels. The few extra years we gain by using environmental unfriendly dirty fuels will not aviod the
coming crisis.

3. Other issues like species extinction, pollution, water quality,
public health, etc. are usually not of urgent interest to most
Americans. We need to focus on one message; we are running out of fossil fuels. The tank is moving toward empty.
Our energy guzzling economy is hurtling down the road
with no hope for refueling. The truth is, if we start to immediately address the fossil fuel depletion problem, many of
the other related environmental problems will become less
serious. Even if we continue on our present path, all fossil
fuel and closely related population problems will eventually
resolve themselves through the harsh laws of depleted resources. Mother Nature will triumph in the end. As just another living species, our remaining descendents will be cru-
elly forced to come to long-term sustainable equilibrium
with the earth's environment and remaining resources.

Sustainability is the environmental buzzword for a steady state
process. To sustain means to maintain, support, and keep alive.
For our purposes and for the future of civilization, we need to find
a balance between energy intake and energy expended. This is
equally true of our own bodies. Each of us is a complex machine
able to convert energy (measured in Calories) from the food we
eat into work. For eons, our ancestors survived by expending
nearly all their energy just to find enough food. In today's age of
easy energy and resulting plentiful food, we each can eat far more
Calories than we need. This leads to obesity and other related ills.

The energy party the industrialized world is now enjoying
helps to explain many disparities and conflicts. Energy is the
difference between modern military might and legions of foot
soldiers. The conspicuous consumption of the western world,
now visible to the third world via modern media, leads to great
animosity. Why do they hate us? Our gross consumption of energy, much of it coming from third world resources, is visible
and alarming to the rest of the world. Modern western

Europeans question American squandering of the world's energy resources, while at the same time they are heavily taxed on fuel for transportation.

This book is an engineer's attempt to envision a model of a low energy sustainable modern lifestyle along with a timely plan to get there. No attempt is made to alienate specific groups who may be liberal or conservative, religious fundamentalists or non-believers. We are all on one lifeboat and must share the resources and pull in unison if there is to be any future worth living. All of us will have to make the necessary changes. These will not be sacrifices since in many cases we will be better off.

Basic science and math clearly show that we must make significant reductions in our energy consumption. Our only hope is to start immediately while we still have enough fossil energy left to make a controlled transition.

---

chapter 2

Energy 101 ...
Energy, Work, Power

Almost all the energy we have has in the past, or presently, continues to flow from the sun onto the surface of the earth. This radiation energy combines the carbon in the short gaseous molecule of carbon dioxide (CO_2) with the hydrogen from water (H_2O) through a process called photosynthesis. Familiar green plant life forms from algae and moss to large trees have been taking in this energy from the sun for billions of years and using it to make larger molecules of hydrogen and carbon commonly referred to as carbohydrates.

Under unique conditions of heat and pressure, some of these carbohydrates were compressed into tightly packed forms of energy like oil and coal, or trapped in pockets of the earth as natural gas. The incredibly long time this process took allowed the earth to be endowed with a substantial amount of concentrated stored energy called fossil hydrocarbons or fossil energy. Our industrial age and concurrent 6-fold (one billion to 6 billion) population explosion in the last 150 years has only been possible because of the extraction and utilization of this previously stored energy.

There are other less concentrated forms of energy including the very dilute continuous inflow of sunshine. These will be discussed later in this chapter. The important point is that modern, industrialized civilization has evolved only because of the availability of an incredible amount of energy. Today, about 86% of this ubiquitous energy comes from finite deposits of previously stored hydrocarbons, which are now rapidly being depleted.

The exceptions to the energy, which came from or is now coming directly from the sun, are moon gravitational pull (tides), geothermal energy (from deep in the earth), and nuclear energy.

Since all forms of energy can do work, they can be converted from one form to a different secondary form, but not without some loss in the conversion. The ratio of the secondary energy to its earlier form is called efficiency. The conversion may be very efficient or very poor depending on the procedure used.

As should be clear by now, energy is the underlying theme of this book. To grasp the complete message, it helps to have a basic understanding of this complex subject. There are many textbooks available but few are easy to understand. An exception in layman's language is entitled, *Energies*, by Vaclav Smil.[1]

In simple terms, I will attempt to provide enough background to better understand my book and help sort out all the conflicting inputs we hear today. This chapter is intended only for reference. In order to appreciate the basic message of fossil energy depletion, it is not necessary to fully understand the technical terms and equations. The exception is to gain at least a numerical appreciation for the huge difference in energy content between different sources. Numbers are also necessary to compare the magnitude of concentrated fossil energy with the relatively puny human, animal, and continuous inflowing solar forms. Understandable equivalent units are necessary to appreciate the original finite endowments of stored hydrocarbon energy and to compare these with usage rates and remaining reserves. Confusion concerning energy is a primary cause of poor decision-making and the lack of urgency that is so prevalent today. Numbers are also necessary if we are to intelligently search for a sustainable future and a realistic plan to get there within an acceptable time frame.

The following basic definitions, energy equivalences, and necessary explanations will be helpful as background for this book or other references:

ENERGY is the ability to do work.

WORK is the movement, of something from one place to another, or the equivalent amount of heat energy required to raise something from one temperature to a higher temperature.

POWER is how fast the work happens or the rate that the energy is being used.

Work (W) can be expressed as a force (F), like a push or a pull, occurring over a distance (D) and in the direction traveled. For instance, if it takes 10 pounds of push or pull to provide enough sliding force to move a sled, and the distance traveled is 50 feet, the force times the distance equals the work.
In equation form:

Force x Distance = Work

With the numbers substituted in our sled example:

10 lbs. x 50 ft. = 500 ft.lbs.

Note, that if a 9 lb. force was exerted against the sled and no movement occurred, no work would be done.

9 lbs. x 0 ft. = 0 ft.lbs.

You could lean (or prop a stick in your place) against the sled all day, the sled would not move and no work would be done.

Work requires both force and distance traveled. Energy, which can be in different forms, is the ability to do the work. Power is how fast the work is done.

There are many ways that the sled could be moved, such as with a snowmobile, a dog team, cross-country skier, a winch with an electric motor, a sail, and many more, but in each case, the sliding work done and energy used is the same, 500 ft.lbs., as long as the sum of the forces resisting movement totals 10 pounds.

If there were wheels on the sled so it rolled and required only 5 pounds of force, then the work done would be 250 ft.lbs. (5 lbs. x 50 ft. = 250 ft.lbs.) The wheel was a great invention to reduce the work of transportation and lessen the required energy.

Energy exists in many different forms, but in each case suggested above, the energy required, or the ability to do the work of overcoming 10 pounds of drag, is still 500 foot pounds. It doesn't matter if the force came from a gasoline engine, an animal, a human, or the wind. Energy is that elusive something able to do the work. The units for energy and work are the same.

At this point, we will leave energy for a minute and discuss power so that we are absolutely clear about the three terms: energy, work, and power.

It doesn't take a great leap of intuition to appreciate that moving the sled in 50 seconds is a much different task than moving it the same 50 feet in five seconds. A dog or person could easily handle the 50-second task, but it would take a snowmobile or a good gust of wind with a big sail to move it the same distance in five seconds. Power is the time rate of doing the work. In equation form:

$$Power = Force \ x \ Distance/Time$$

Our original slow sled example becomes:

$$P = 10 \ lbs. \ x \ 50 \ ft./50 \ sec. = 10 \ ft.lbs./sec.$$

In the faster example such as with wind or snowmobile:

P = 10 lbs. x 50 ft./5 sec. = 100 ft.lbs./sec.

This is ten times as much power as the slower example.

The work in each case is the same, but the power is ten times greater because the time (T) to do the work changed from a task we could easily do ourselves slowly to a ten times quicker task requiring a machine stronger than most humans. Remember, the work done and the energy used while moving between two points, no matter what the time, is the same assuming the sliding friction remains the same in each case.

If we're in a hurry, we need more power. A stronger machine or an athlete can do the same work as the weaker but in less time. Power is a measure of the effort within a specific time period.

A common English unit for power is horsepower (Hp). By definition one horsepower equals 550 ft.lbs. of work done in one second. To introduce horsepower to our above slower sled problem:

10 ft.lbs./sec. divided by 550 ft.lbs. per second (per Hp)
= 0.018 Hp

In the faster case, the horsepower is:

100 ft.lbs./sec. divided by 550 ft.lbs. per second (per Hp)
= 0.18 Hp

In real life, as speed increases, the air resistance will start to be a significant drag factor in addition to the sliding friction. Air resistance is a squared factor. Even though it might be negligible at slow speeds it increases four fold each time the speed doubles.

In the second case, when moving the sled ten times as fast, the air resistance would be 10^2 or 100 times greater and in theory start to add to the sliding friction depending on the speed, shape, and the frontal area of the sled. Together, air resistance plus sliding friction make up a total drag force (F) and the amount of work (F x D) required to move the sled. This is why a streamlined shape becomes so important at high speed. Air resistance explains why moving things in a hurry is much more energy intensive. However, in our sled examples, the faster case of a 50-foot distance in 5 seconds is 10 ft./sec., or only about 7 mph (miles per hour). This is still slow enough that air drag is insignificant compared to the sliding friction so it can be ignored.

The energy to overcome air resistance starts to become important above about 15 mph. At higher speeds movement through air becomes the very dominate drag force resisting most of the work (energy).

In order to complete this short review of energy, work, and power, we need to clarify different forms of energy as well as to gain a quantitative understanding of the amount of work each can do.

MECHANICAL ENERGY

To review traditional mechanical terms described above:

Work = distance times force = foot pounds

Energy is equivalent to work = foot pounds

Power = work divided by time = foot pounds per second

THERMAL (THE SUBJECT OF HEAT) ENERGY

To raise a mass of material a certain temperature also requires energy. Therefore, work, the energy required, and the temperature increase of a substance are equivalent. I will try to clarify this concept with a few definitions:

The familiar term BTU (British Thermal Unit) is the amount of energy (or work) required to raise one pound of water one degree Fahrenheit; for example:
To heat one gallon (about 8 pounds) of water fifty degrees would require:

8 lbs. x 50°f = 400 BTU

The BTU is a term of energy (or work) just like a foot pound. One BTU is directly equivalent to 778 foot pounds.

In metric terms, one calorie is the amount of energy (or work) required to raise one gram of water one degree centigrade. For instance:

To heat the same gallon of water as above, which weighs 8 pounds (3632 grams), 50°f (27.8°c) would require:

3632 grams times 27.8°c equals 100,970 calories

Obviously one calorie is not very big, so scientists sometime use the kilocalorie (1000 calories) especially as a measure of energy value of food. When this is done, a capital C may be used (not to be confused with temperature in degrees centigrade, °c).

Thermal energy may also be the output of a chemical reaction. This occurs when the complex carbon molecules of fuel combine with oxygen to make heat (thermal energy) and simpler, lower energy, carbon molecules like carbon dioxide (CO_2) or carbon monoxide (CO). This process is called burning or combustion.

The minimum food energy required by a healthy adult in one day is about 2000 kilocalories. Humans are very complex machines requiring large quantities of sophisticated fuels. All basic carbohydrate fuel sources provide about 4 kilocalories/gram of energy. The average requirement of 2000 kilocalories per day per person equals 500 grams (just over one pound) of carbohydrates per day or about 400 pounds per year. Proteins have about the same caloric energy value and may be a substitute for carbohydrate energy. Fats have two to three times the energy value of carbohydrates.

Further reference about kilocalorie counting for food is available on the Nutrient, Data Laboratory website (www.nal.usda.gov).

15

We can now see why food production, as the fuel source for our bodies, is the primary energy concern for any society. It takes considerable energy (fossil fuel, animal power, and/or human power) to produce 400 pounds of food per year per person. With today's energy intensive modern agriculture, 10 to 20 kilocalories are used to deliver one kilocalorie of food to the dinner table. Without the fossil fuels or some other alternative source of more concentrated energy, we will have to go back to subsistence, lower yield, agriculture using human and animal power to provide our food.

Now that we have enough basics of scientific terms and quantification of energy, we can better appreciate the astonishing energy content of fossil fuels and reject inaccurate or misleading information. Consider the following facts straight from any technical source book, and compare the different concentrated energy sources with the feeble output of human labor.

One gallon of oil, kerosene, diesel fuel, gasoline, fat, etc. (they're all about the same) has the concentrated combustion energy of approximately 150,000 BTU. This is a tremendous amount of stored energy and represents the ability (before efficiency losses) to do over one hundred and sixteen million foot pounds (150,000 BTU per gallon x 778 ft.lbs. per BTU = 116,700,000 ft.lbs. per gallon) of work. We can go down to the corner gas station and buy this amount of fuel (energy) for about $1.50. Working at a typical continuous maximum of 256 BTU per hour of power (75 watts), hour after hour, a strong healthy adult would have to work 600 hours to equal this amount of energy. No wonder we live in a age of comparatively "free" energy. Even if the fuel were converted into work at a 25 percent efficiency rate (typical for fossil fuel energy), it would still take 150 hours of steady manual labor to equal the energy in a gallon of fossil fuel.

At $1.50/gal. for gasoline, equivalent human labor to do the same work is worth about one cent per hour.

A similar analysis reveals that a pound of coal with 10,000 BTU is equal to about 10 hours of manual labor and a pound of

16

dry wood with 5,000 BTU per pound contains energy equal to five hours of constant manual labor.

ELECTRICAL ENERGY

Unfortunately, for the average person trying to understand the subject of energy, the electrical community has still another set of terms for energy, work, and power. The electrical engineer starts with the basic concept:

Volts (the force, or push, like pounds in mechanical terms) times the current (in units of amperes or the quantity of electrons flowing at the speed of light) equals watts (power).

Volts x Amps = Watts

Since we have force, distance, and time (understood as speed of light), we have power. The watt (or kilowatts as thousands of watts) is the fundamental unit of electrical power in both English and metric systems. The equivalence of electrical and mechanical power is defined as:

746 watts (0.746 kw) = one horsepower

One kilowatt and three fourths of a horsepower are similar in magnitude. In Europe, cars are rated in kilowatts instead of horsepower. Since a kilowatt is a unit of power, it must be multiplied by time to get back to the simpler concepts of work and energy like foot pounds. The common product of kilowatts times hours is a measure of how much we pay for electrical energy coming into our homes from the utility grid.

One kilowatt (power) times one hour = one kilowatt hour, or

1 kw x 1 hr. = 1 kwh

In your monthly electrical bill, you will see that electrical energy (not the power) costs about 15 cents per kilowatt-hour. A typical household may use about 700 kwh per month for about $105.00. This is an incredible bargain unique to our modern, low cost energy, industrialized civilization.

A strong human working a complete 40 hour week can only produce 75 watts of power times 40 hours, which is equal to 3000 watt hours (3 kwh) each week. This is equivalent to the thermal energy required to heat one hot shower. At electrical costs of 15 cents per kwh, a week of hard human work would be worth about 45 cents, about one cent per hour.

The above technical background is all we need to understand the remainder of this book and the magnitude of the situation we've gotten into in just the last 150 years. Consider a brief flashback in history:

5000BC   About this time, human beings came out of the woods or savannahs as hunter/gatherers in delicate balance with nature and started to grow a little excess food energy in the form of grains. This slight surplus of energy beyond the minimum required for survival allowed the beginning of civilization. In addition, beasts of burden were domesticated to add to the amount of work that humans alone could do as well as provide concentrated food energy as meat and milk. The agricultural revolution allowed humans to stop moving about, build villages, and multiply in population one hundred fold from about 10 million to almost a billion by the start of the industrial age. This early age of grain-energy reached a peak when the expansion and military might of Rome extended to the limits that grain production could support. The use of slave labor also provided incremental energy to do additional work. This practice with its detestable human rights issue is common right into the fossil fuel era beginning 150 years ago and even to the present in some parts of the world.

500 AD   Non-fossil fuel machines like water wheels and windmills were built to further energy availability and give another small boost to civilization and leisure time.

1500   Civilization continued to grow slowly until wood, which was the major source of fuel for energy needs, began to be seriously depleted. Fortunately, the first use of fossil fuels in the forms of coal and peat satisfied ever increasing energy demands and kept the quality of life gradually improving. During this period the whale population was almost decimated in a few decades for the oil to be used in lighting more extravagant homes.

1775 James Watt (1736-1819) invented the steam engine and ushered in the industrial age by improving on the piston pump used for removing water from coal mines. This wondrous machine allowed the conversion of concentrated, previously stored energy, such as wood and coal, into work and power far in excess of what man, beast, windmill, or waterwheel could do.

1859 About the time of the Civil War when coal driven locomotives and steamships were already well established, Colonel Edwin Drake struck plentiful crude oil in Pennsylvania. This drilling technology was rapidly followed by further discoveries in the U.S. and then eventually worldwide. Liquid crude oil eventually supplanted coal as the number one fossil fuel energy source because of its ease of procurement, transportation, and utilization in machines which could convert its huge energy content into useful work.

1900 Beginning about a century ago, inventors found many new ways to harness the concentrated energy of free flowing oil and cleaner derivatives like kerosene and gasoline. All types of machines evolved to power industry, agriculture, and especially transportation for military, personal, and commercial use on land, sea, and in the air. There are centenarians alive today that span this entire era. It is no small coincidence that the 100-year anniversary of the airplane exactly coincides with this hydrocarbon energy epoch.

The tremendous power requirements to move large masses quickly over long distances can only be provided by fossil fuels. The only exceptions are concentrated biofuels and liquid hydrogen, both requiring even larger energy inputs for their formation than they return for useful work.

1950   The use of fossil fuels including natural gas to make hydrogen culminated in more recent years as rocket fuel. This is the only way to provide the awesome power required to propel objects outward against the pull of the very strong force of earth's gravitational field. (The use of hydrogen as a concentrated fuel in lieu of fossil fuel will be discussed in more detail in other parts of this book.)

At this point I will summarize the units and equivalents used for energy, work, and power into one table sufficient for understanding the remainder of this book and other references. Wherever possible, mechanical energy, electrical energy, and work will be quantified as kilowatt-hours, and power will be in kilowatts. Thermal energy will be referred to in terms of BTU's or equivalent billion barrels of oil (EBBO), with each barrel containing 42 gallons or 6,300,000 BTU's worth of energy. Keep in mind that the total thermal energy of a fossil fuel cannot be converted directly to useful electrical energy, mechanical energy, or work without an energy loss. A 25% efficiency factor for internal combustion engines and 35% for electric power plants will be used where appropriate to calculate the equivalent fossil fuel energy. In other words, usable, secondary electrical or mechanical output is divided by the efficiency to find the required primary energy. For instance a ten kilowatt photovoltaic system would equal a fossil fuel power plant input of 10/0.35 or 28.57 kilowatts equal to 97,486 BTU/hr.

SUMMARY OF EQUIVALENTS AND UNITS:

$1000 = 10^3$ = thousand (or kilo, K)
$1,000,000 = 10^6$ = million (or mega, M)
$1,000,000,000 = 10^9$ = billion (or giga, G)
$1,000,000,000,000 = 10^{12}$ = trillion (or tera, T)
$1,000,000,000,000,000 = 10^{15}$ = quadrillion (or peta, P)

Energy (or work equivalent)

1 kwh = 3412 BTU

1 barrel of oil = 1846 kwh = 6.3 x 10⁶ (million) BTU

1 kilocalorie = 3.968 BTU

1 BTU = 778 foot pounds

1 foot pound = 1.356 Joules (Newton meters)

1 BTU = 0.252 kilocalories

1 kwh = 860 kilocalories

1 kwh = 2.65 x 10⁶ (million) foot pounds

1 gallon hydrocarbon fuel = 150,000 BTU

1 pound high quality coal = 10,000 BTU

1 pound dry wood = 5,000 BTU

    (wet wood may have zero energy value)

1 cubic meter (36 cubic feet) natural gas = 36,000 BTU

1 cubic foot natural gas = 1,000 BTU

1 trillion (10^{12}) cubic meters natural gas = 36 quadrillion (10^{15}) BTU

1 trillion (10^{12}) cubic meters natural gas = 5.72 EBBO

    (equivalent billion barrels of oil)

1 quadrillion (10^{15}) BTU = 0.159 EBBO

Power

1 horsepower (Hp) = 550 foot pounds/second (ft.lbs./sec.)

1 kw = 1.34 Hp

1 Hp = 746 watts (0.746 kw)

1 kw = 0.95 BTU/sec.

1 Hp = 0.71 BTU/sec.

1 watt = 1 Joule/sec. = 1 Newton meter/sec.

    (metric terms used for power)

There are several directly related subjects, which are pertinent to understanding energy:

SOLAR

Incoming solar energy is our best hope for an acceptable industrialized future. It is clean and ubiquitous but dilute. Solar energy arrives at the earth's surface as radiation from nuclear fusion in the sun. The maximum power intensity that this energy flows in perpendicular to the earth's surface is a rate of about one kilowatt per square meter (10.9 square feet) of surface area. Because of efficiency losses, the actual availability of this power is significantly less. With optimal conditions, photovoltaic cells will convert only about one tenth of this solar power to electricity or 100 watts per square meter. (100 watts = 1/10 kilowatt) Non electrical but active or passive solar heating for hot water or residential heating can be up to twice this amount (200 watts/m^2) under ideal conditions. In real life, the total usable solar power varies greatly with latitude and hours of unimpeded sunlight. Typical useful solar energy for electricity or heating is between 2 to 8 hours per day. This is called insolation or equivalent hours of full direct sunlight. The actual, useable energy would therefore vary from 200 wh per day to 800 wh per day for each square meter of solar panel.

One very important fact to remember as we move to a civilization fueled by incoming solar energy is the considerable energy required to melt and process the silicon into photovoltaic cells. Initially, this input energy was more than the cell would produce in its lifetime. With steady improvements, this pay back period can now be lower than one year, which means that it takes less than the first year of electrical output to return the energy to make the solar cells. Of course, this manufacturing energy now comes from fossil fuels, but eventually as we run out of fossil fuels the photovoltaic manufacturing process will have to provide its own energy for production.

WIND

Another form of solar energy is from air movement caused by solar heating and cooling of the atmosphere. The available energy from wind impinging on a rotating blade attached to a generator will vary greatly depending on wind speed and blade design. A typical value (similar to photovoltaic power) is 100 watts per square meter of swept blade area. Again, like all solar energy, a considerable amount of fossil fuel is needed, to make the blades, generators, towers, etc. In a fossil fuel free civilization, all of this manufacturing energy will have to come from the renewable sources.

BIOMASS

A third form of solar energy is the photosynthesis of bio (living) mass. Everything green in nature indicates the conversion by incoming solar radiation of CO_2 into more concentrated, carbon molecules that can be used as fuel. As pointed out earlier, biomass in various forms was a source of civilization's energy requirements for thousands of years. The problems with overdependence on biomass (primarily wood) are many. Obviously, it takes proper soils, water, and time to grow the organic fuel. Wood was seriously depleted in the Middle Ages for fuel and construction. We've had a reprieve in some areas with the advent of the fossil fuel age, but more likely, the availability of fossil fuels has encouraged serious continued depletion all over the world from the rainforests of the tropics to the heavily forested temperate zones. One example of an all-out assault on the earth's resources is to use rapidly dwindling fossil fuels to cut, chip, transport, and process wood to generate additional electricity referred to as renewable "green" energy. Wood is not truly a renewable energy if we do not follow a very careful plan to conserve our forests and if fossil fuel energy is required for harvest and transport. In Chapter 7, I describe a microcosm of the depletion of biomass as it occurred on Easter Island.

HYDROELECTRIC

The sun's energy warms the air which evaporates water in the oceans. Warm air rises and carries the water vapor to higher, colder elevations where the moisture is squeezed out and returns to the earth in familiar forms of precipitation. During the gravitational flow back to lower surfaces, water accumulates and can provide significant energy to generators conveniently placed at dams, which control flow quantity and direction. Hydroelectric power is the best bargain in the energy spectrum although fish and locally displaced people may not agree. It is clean and sustainable. It does not rely on finite fuel sources, except as required to build and maintain the dams and generators. It would appear that hydropower would satisfy the future needs of a sustainable civilization. It does, but only where the water flow is adequate and most of the accessible sites have already been utilized. Today, about 7% of the total energy in the world comes from "hydro" and even that amount is not entirely dependable because of the weather. Between 1996 and 2001, the U.S. experienced a 40% decline in hydroelectric output because of drought conditions (which may be caused by global warming). Another indication of the limitations of hydroelectric power is that it has decreased from providing about 40% of our total electric generating capacity in 1930 to about 3% in 2001.

NUCLEAR

Just after the beginning of the 20th century, Albert Einstein proposed that mass and energy are equivalent. This is shown in the familiar equation: $E = MC^2$ where E is energy, M is mass, and C, the third term, is the speed of light. (186,000 miles/sec). Only certain isotopes (rare higher molecular weight atoms) of scarce materials like uranium can be used to fuel a nuclear bomb or power plant. The only proven process is called fission, which releases great amounts of deadly radiation as a byproduct. Contaminated materials and spent fuels must be carefully secured and stored. As recently as 1970, nuclear power was expected to be the panacea for an energy-addicted civilization. Subsequent disasters at Three Mile Island in Pennsylvania (March, 1979) and Chernobyl in the Ukraine (April, 1986) completely turned public and considerable scientific opinion against this direction. Today, some countries (France) continue to carefully produce a large share of their electrical power from the fission of uranium. In the U.S., about 20% of our electrical power and 8% of our total power comes from nuclear energy. There is talk in the present Bush administration of increasing our reliance on nuclear energy, but the problems of waste disposal have not been solved, and even if all the environmental hazards could be accepted, the fuel sources are finite and were heavily mined during the Cold War. The World Nuclear Association[2] paints a rosy picture about the future of fission and uranium sources. We must continue to keep in mind, however, that the mining of uranium is very environmentally destructive and requires huge amounts of fossil fuel to extract, move, and process. Eventually, nuclear energy will also have to provide its own up-front energy to be truly sustainable. How will the earthmoving and processing equipment be fueled?

Nuclear fusion, like the sun, is the Holy Grail of energy and is being offered as the hope for an ultra high tech civilization. To date, after many years and billions of dollars of research, we don't seem to be any closer to a practical power plant. Maybe, if we could keep our industrialized civilization going for another 150 years, we could find a path to a fusion-powered world (other than the old reliable sun).

OTHER ENERGY SOURCES

There are several other energy sources that are either in use, development, or have some relevance. These are geothermal, which utilizes the heat under the surface of the earth; and tidal, which uses the gravitational pull of the moon to harness tidal water flow. There have even been proposals for harnessing the difference in seawater density between the surface and very low depths and converting this flow into generated electricity. There is a surge of activity for harvesting wave power. These are highly localized sites or speculative technology and to date have little effect on our total energy requirements.

HYDROGEN

The proposal of hydrogen[3,4,5,6,7,8] as the fuel of the future and solution to our coming energy crisis is misleading and dangerous because it gives a false sense of optimism. Liquid hydrogen has a very high thermal energy content of 61,000 BTU per pound

25

compared to about 18,000 BTU per pound for common liquid fuels, but the problems with hydrogen are many:

- It is a very flammable light gas and requires extremely high pressures (about 5000 pounds per square inch) or very cold temperatures (minus 400°F) to liquefy it for storage or shipment. Compare these hurdles to today's procedures and safeguards necessary for bottled propane at about 200 psi.
- It is a very common element but exists chemically bound with oxygen as water or with carbon in fossil fuels. It also appears in many other chemical compounds but always combined tightly with other elements and requiring considerable energy for separation.
- Of all hydrogen used today, about 97% comes from fossil fuels (primarily natural gas) and 3% from electrolysis of water. What sense does it make to use our finite fuel sources just to make a different form of energy? In the case of electrolysis, it takes more energy to separate the hydrogen than is returned when the hydrogen recombines with oxygen. When hydrogen is made from the high temperature stripping of natural gas considerable provision must also be made for the disposal of the resulting (sequestered) CO_2.

For practical purposes, hydrogen is a misleading issue in our coming fossil fuel crisis. It is difficult to believe that it can be proposed as the solution. Our decision makers hear optimistic predictions about hydrogen and divert attention from the real problem, the finite reserves and depletion of fossil fuels.

The best hydrogen can do is to provide a very exotic, expensive storage medium (like a super battery). The stored energy density by weight of liquid hydrogen at 5,000 psi is three times higher than that for liquid fossil fuels, but this is offset by the weight of the high-pressure container and four times larger volume required. Hydrogen fueled cars and airplanes have been prototyped for many years, but cost and complexity have limited these efforts to technical oddities with huge expensive fuel tanks. In April 1988 the Soviet hydrogen fueled TU-154 jetliner used a large portion of the fuselage for the hydrogen storage tank to power just one of three engines.

Supporters of hydrogen refer to this experiment to argue that hydrogen can fuel commercial and military aviation without clarifying the compromises that have to be made.

It is true that liquid hydrogen can be a source of concentrated energy similar to fossil fuels. In a totally fossil fuel free civilization and with electricity available only from renewable sources, liquid hydrogen may be the only concentrated energy source other than biofuels when and where requirements cannot be served by batteries or a long extension cord. Examples might be an agricultural tractor or construction machine requiring huge amounts of power to build a dam or extract uranium. A typical 25 kw (33 Hp) tractor, similar to a small 2-plow farm tractor, could be fueled at the farm with hydrogen produced from photovoltaic electricity. At one kw peak power from each ten square meter grid, a 250 m^2 (about 50 feet by 50 feet) array would provide one hour of tractor power at full power for every hour the grid is exposed to direct sunlight. This is equivalent to two gallons of diesel fuel or gasoline burned at 25% efficiency. Such a photovoltaic array alone would cost $100,000 at today's prices. This is in addition to the hydrogen handling equipment and fuel cell-electric drive complexity if used instead of a conventional piston engine. Battery powered tractors and even draft animals seem more realistic. By the same thinking, a typical 100 kw bulldozer would require four times greater investment in photovoltaics and hydrogen handling equipment, but it may be the only way to do heavy earth moving. We will still need petroleum based lubricants, hydraulics, and plastics or rely on substitutes made from refined biomaterials.

Still, billions of dollars are being awarded to fund hydrogen research. A large part of this investment would be better spent to develop energy independent personal residences and electric vehicles for the future as well as to subsidize and encourage the conservation of the fuel we have left. Comprehensive analyses of hydrogen problems can be found in "Why Hydrogen is No Solution", "Much Ado About Nothing" and downloaded from *From This Wilderness* newsletters.[9]

chapter 3

Where Are We Now?
A Situation Analysis

Including World and U.S. Energy Consumption, and References

Our short fossil fuel era is defined by previously stored energy. For hundreds of millions of years organisms lived and died and were subsequently compressed with heat into a solid, liquid, or gas, which were buried into layers of the earth's crust. This concentration of hydrocarbons resulted in stored energy, the basis for our modern industrial age. Fossil fuels are not abundant throughout the world. An excellent, in depth, analysis of how oil is formed, where to look for it, and how much is left can be found in the book, *Hubbert's Peak*,[1] written by Kenneth Deffeyes, a life long petroleum geologist and professor emeritus of Princeton University. Another new book, *The Essence of Oil & Gas Depletion*,[2] has just been published by Colin Campbell, the recognized world leader on this subject. This comprehensive book describes in detail the oil production history and projected reserves for every important country (see Appendix 5). It also includes timely updates of many aspects of the title subject. Quoting from the back cover of Campbell's book:

Oil and gas are finite fossil fuels from the geological past that are inevitably subject to depletion. Eventually we must run out, but what matters more is the inevitable peak of production when growth gives way to decline. The wider implications of this historic discontinuity are colossal.

In recent years, experts have learned how to more accurately quantify how much fossil fuel we have used and how much is left. After starting with coal, which is the most accessible, we are now rapidly consuming the cleanest and most available oil and natural gas. All three forms can be used somewhat interchangeably. Heavier forms of oil and coal can be converted to gaseous or liquid forms, although with attendant energy input and pollution.

In order to combine information from many sources into a quantitative and more understandable format, I will use the following methodology:

1. Start with total world energy consumption in all forms; fossil fuels, nuclear, and renewable.
2. Convert all energy forms to equivalent barrels of oil. Because of the huge quantities involved, the common term used will be equivalent billion barrels of oil (EBBO). If electrical output is the quantitative value of energy such as from a nuclear plant, a hydroelectric dam, solar cells, or a wind farm, the electrical output in kilowatts will be divided by an efficiency factor of 35% (0.35). This equals the equivalent billion barrels of oil (EBBO) that would be required to produce the same amount of electricity in a conventional power plant.
3. Use Department of Energy-Energy Information Agency (DOE-EIA)[3] statistics as the primary reference for past and present energy production and consumption in the U.S. and throughout the world.
4. Refer to other sources as needed for verification and analysis of remaining reserves.

From this information, the big picture is clear. We have become hooked on plentiful fossil energy, but time is running out.

Earlier authors have anticipated the problem,[4,5,6,7] but surplus Middle East oil has kept us in a state of energy euphoria. Now the picture is becoming clearer. We are reaching and going over the peak of available resources and looking at the downhill side. Jeremy Rifkin calls this, "sliding down Hubbert's Bell Curve," in Chapter 2 of his book, *The Hydrogen Economy*.[8] For our analysis, I will intentionally de-emphasize the remaining coal and nonconventional types of oil in the form of shale oil and tar sand. There are loose estimates of reserves of these forms of fossil fuels, equal to hundreds of billions of barrels of oil, but they require huge amounts of energy to process, and cause considerable environmental problems both in extraction and refining. Global warming and pollution will be even more serious as we inevitably are forced to accelerate dependence on these less desirable forms of concentrated fossil energy. As we struggle to reach a worldwide sustainable energy future, these last forms of fossil fuel will be our final chance to continue a modicum of industrialized civilization. If we don't count them in our pocket now, we will have more incentive to start immediately to make the necessary reductions in oil and natural gas usage.

We will need all remaining forms of fossil energy for agriculture, national defense, modern healthcare, plastics, lubricants, hydraulics, absolutely necessary transportation, etc. We need to play a mind game and pretend the dirtier fuels are not available until we absolutely need them.

The following finite resource consumption curves show world oil consumption to date. This visual display is from page 5 of *Hubbert's Peak*.[1] Also shown on the same coordinates, is U.S. oil production to date (from pages 143 and 155 of the same book). It is interesting to note that U.S. production, which is well past the peak at about 1971, lies exactly on the expected bell-shaped probability curve that world production will soon follow. See Appendix 5 for A Numeric Summary of World Past Production and Remaining Reserves. The dotted

World and U.S. Oil Consumption Through 2001

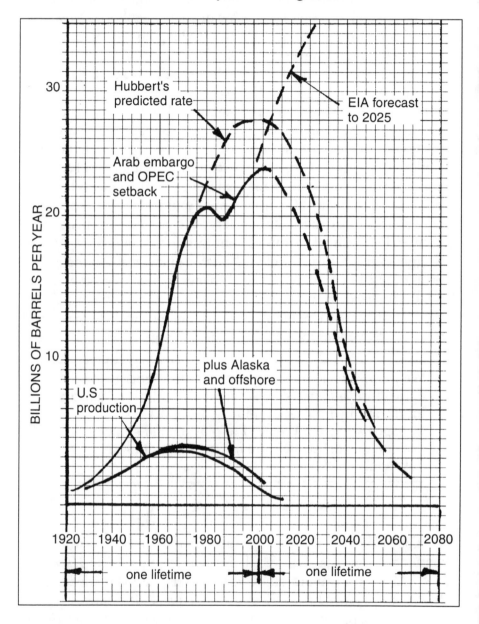

line continuing upward is the Energy Information Agency (EIA) forecast to the year 2025. This gross disparity between the petroleum experts and optimistic governmental projections is extremely important for our understanding of fossil energy and will be discussed further throughout this book.

The original, total U.S. endowment of oil was 220 billion barrels of which 200 billion barrels have already been used. This leaves 20 billion barrels left unused in the U.S. At over 6 billion barrels consumed annually, we have only a three-year supply of our own oil left. The U.S. Geological Survey (USGS) estimates that an additional 7 billion barrels of recoverable oil may be in the Alaskan National Wildlife Refuge (ANWR), enough for one-year consumption in the U.S. at the present rate. It would be folly for us to use this now when it will be so precious for our children. They'll wonder what we were thinking of when we wasted energy as we do today.

Of the original 2,000 billion barrel total endowment of world oil, about 1,000 billion barrels of oil have been used. Most experts (including those in British Petroleum and Royal Dutch Shell) agree that there are about 1,000 billion barrels left. We are half full (or half empty), but most of our consumption has been in the last 25 years. At the 2002 world consumption rate of 28.5 EBBO annually we will be out of oil in 36 years (see Appendix 5).

At this point, I will focus on the huge disagreement over the quantity of remaining reserves. The oil experts like Deffeyes[1] and Campbell[2] are telling us loud and clear, "We're going over the peak." They can predict this well in advance by analyzing the ratio of new discoveries to consumption. This ratio is already in serious decline, a warning of the end for any finite reserve. This obvious mathematical prediction is totally at odds with the international energy outlook to 2025 as reported by the EIA.[3]

The EIA predicts in their 25 year forecast, shown extended beyond the above consumption curves, that world total energy production (including oil) will increase 58 percent by the year

2025. Oil production will increase from 25 EBBO to 42 EBBO per year. For this to happen the world would use 805 EBBO of oil in the next 25 years. If production then continued at a constant level from 2025 to 2043, we would use an additional 756 EBBO for a total consumption of 1.56 trillion barrels in the next 40 years, all from a reserve of one trillion barrels.

Someone is dead wrong on a very important disagreement. On such an important issue, it would seem prudent to err on the conservative side.

What difference does it make anyway, whether we have 30 or 50 years of oil left. The crisis facing us is still the same.

Natural gas reserves are difficult to quantify especially in less friendly countries, but they appear to be similar to or little better than for petroleum. World reserves are presently estimated at 155 trillion cubic meters, or an equivalent 884 EBBO. World natural gas consumption rate is 14 EBBO per year; therefore we would appear to have a 63-year reserve to production ratio (884 EBBO divided by 14 EBBO equals 63 years). Sixty-three years may seem like a long time, but this time period will be considerably reduced as consumption is increased. This is inevitable as petroleum becomes more expensive and especially if natural gas is stripped for a hydrogen economy or used to process tar sand. The EIA estimates natural gas usage will double in the next 25 years. Canada now sends over half of its natural gas to the U.S. but production is in decline.

Regardless of which estimates are used, we are talking about depleting nearly all of the world's oil and natural gas in far less than the lifetime of a child born in 2003.

As we go through 2003, even the above forecasts may be considerably optimistic. U.S. natural gas production has declined to an annual rate of 524 billion cubic meters (3 EBBO). In this same period, wholesale prices have more than triples from about $2.00 per thousand cubic feet to over $6.00. John Wood, the director of the EIA in Dallas, says that the higher prices will increase exploration and supply. Michael Zenker, a senior director at Cambridge Energy Research Associates, counters that our cornerstone of gas supplies along the Gulf Coast is petering out. "We're having a tough enough time keeping up with declines from existing fields."[9]

Like oil, there is some disagreement about natural gas reserves, but remember, this is the same natural gas proposed to fuel a future hydrogen economy. We're having trouble now just satisfying electrical and heating demands. Shortfalls of natural gas are already disrupting U.S. economy because liquified natural gas (LNG) can only be landed at four U.S. ports.

At this point, I will return to an analysis of present (as of 2001) production of all energy sources. Since this is being written in 2003, all U.S. production of 15.5 EBBO in 2001 will be rounded upwards to 16 EBBO. Oil, with a 39% share of total energy, is the primary fossil fuel source being depleted today. The second and third sources are coal and natural gas, each providing about the same 23% share. Together, the big three: oil, coal, and natural gas, provide 86% of the world's energy.[3] From the DOE statistics, we can find the contribution of each energy source in the world and the U.S. for 2001.

	WORLD		USA	
Oil	39%	24.88 EBBO	39%	6.05 EBBO
Natural gas	23%	14.8	24%	3.69
Coal	24%	15.25	23%	3.55
Hydroelectric	6.7%	4.27	3%	0.50
				(0.62 in 1996)
Nuclear	6.6%	4.21	8%	1.20
All other forms	<1%	0.49	3%	0.55
Total in 2001	64 EBBO		15.5 EBBO (in 2001)	
			16.0 (est. in 2003)	

"All other forms" in the above table includes wood, waste, solar, wind, geothermal, and tidal. A close examination of the above numbers shows some inconsistencies depending on which EIA source is used. For purposes of this book, direct electrical energy production from non fossil fuel sources (hydro, nuclear, solar, and wind) will be divided by a 0.35 (35%) efficiency factor to find comparable, equivalent billion barrels of oil (EBBO). As stated earlier, the 15.5 total consumption in 2001 is estimated to increase to 16.0 in 2003 as this book goes to press.

Of the 13.29 EBBO of fossil fuels consumed in the U.S in 2001, approximately 5% (0.59 EBBO) is for non-fuel use (not including liquid petroleum gas) such as asphalt, petrochemicals, plastics, lubricants, etc. These represent some of the thousands of ubiquitous fossil fuel uses (including hydrogen production) that we take for granted in this short fossil fuel age. They are typical of the products that will become very dear as we move into a post-industrial age. Another critical need for fossil fuels is for national defense. In 2001, almost 1% (0.123 EBBO) of fossil fuels was used by the Department of Defense (DOD) with 72% of that used for jet fuel.

In the set of curves shown next, I've combined all world and U.S. energy consumption from the earlier table into similar bell shaped curves. These show we are at the top of Hubbert's Peak as the whole world (led predominately by the U.S.) sits on the energy age bubble. It is possible to put both U.S. and world consumption onto exactly the same curves just by changing the Y-coordinate by a factor of four. This is because world consumption is four times that of the U.S. for all major sources even though the U.S. has only one twentieth the population.

If a picture is worth a thousand words, these consumption curves show our present precarious position, how fast we got here and the typical expected resource decline for all fossil fuel sources. We are facing drastic changes in the time frame of our and our children's lives. There is no easy way out of this dilemma. Our only hope for an acceptable future lifestyle is to address this situation immediately. Many authors and scientists have been calling for action, but little is happening.

World and U.S. Energy Consumption from All Sources
(from the table on page 35)

EQUIVALENT BILLION BARRELS OF OIL PER YEAR (EBBO)

(U.S. only)

all energy sources

expected decline of finite resources

oil, natural gas, and coal

oil and natural gas

oil only

one lifetime

one lifetime

37

A tragedy of our civilization is that, in the last 20 years in spite of cries for conservation, we have continued blindly in the wrong direction. Our leaders have acquiesed to the short term gratification of constituents and even encouraged fossil fuel consumption. Many European countries have recognized the challenge. Initiatives have been introduced in Germany and Italy to install solar panels on 10,000 homes. There is legislation pending in England to require 20% of electrical production be from wind by the year 2020. For decades European countries have had much higher gasoline taxation to discourage excessive consumption.

There are many think tanks and administrative agencies, attempting to address the question of how much fossil fuel we have left. Although they do not agree on the exact quantities of fossil fuel reserves, most agree we are dealing with finite resources, and will eventually run short. A partial list later in this chapter summarizes a website search of this subject. Close examination of many of these websites shows a common agreement of about one trillion barrels of oil remaining in the world, enough for 36 years at the 2003 rate of consumption, but not the increased consumption forecast by the EIA. Natural gas reserves show a similar time frame for depletion especially if consumption is increased.

A glaring symbol of excessive energy consumption, and how the U.S. public has been kept from the facts in order to provide short-term profits can be found in the ubiquitous sport utility vehicle (SUV). The book, *High and Mighty* by Keith Bradsher,[10] primarily emphasizes the poor safety record of these vehicles rather than their dismal fuel economy. Bradsher also explains the politics that allowed these popular means of personal transportation to be considered as trucks and thus avoid the mandated fuel economy for automobiles. With over 70 million SUV's produced in the last fifteen years, the increased fuel (the difference between 18 mpg and 28 mpg) they've consumed in that time period (about

0.44 EBBO per year) is about equal to that estimated to be in ANWR and about two and a half times our annual, total car and light truck fuel consumption of 2.6 EBBO (0.44 EBBO/yr x 15 years = 6.6 EBBO). See www.bts.gov (Bureau of Transportation) for specifics of U.S. fuel consumption by various vehicles.[11] History may show that the SUV saga was the culminating chapter in the Industrial Age. We almost turned the corner of conservation in the early '80s, but then embarked on another 20 years of steadily increasing fuel consumption.

It does not seem wise for any politician to discuss a subject regarding environment or energy. People don't like to hear disturbing predictions and make personal adjustments. Ten years ago, Al Gore wrote a most prophetic book, *The Earth in Balance*[12]. His message was lost in the prosperous last decade when the SUV and Hummer became kings of the road.

CHAPTER SUMMARY

It has been a most revealing and daunting task to summarize and make understandable something so complex as world and U.S. energy statistics. There is overwhelming information available especially from the Internet. There are so many different organizations manipulating the numbers that one hand may not know what the other is doing. Very few, especially in the U.S. government information alphabet soup of agencies (DOE, EIA, DOT, and the BTS: Department of Energy, Energy Information Administration and Department of Transportation, Bureau of Transportation Statistics) discuss the energy shortfall of the future.

Other groups are attempting to project a clearer message and sound an alarm, and they do not agree with the optimistic forecasts of the DOE. Several organizations are:

- **The World Watch Institute**[13]

  Quoting their mission statement, "By providing compelling, accessible, and fact based analysis of critical global issues. World Watch informs people around the world about the complex interactions between people, nature, and economics. World Watch focuses on the underlying causes of and practical solutions to the world problems ... etc."

- **The Center for Energy and Environmental Studies**[14] (in conjunction with scientists for a sustainable future and the National Academy of Sciences)

  On May 18, 2001 this prestigious organization published an open (electronic) letter in an attempt to convey a sense of urgency regarding energy. Their website shows this letter and the names of hundreds of distinguished scientists and educators who stand behind the messages relating to the subject of finite fossil fuels, the folly of drilling in ANWR, the problems with nuclear fuel, and the subject of climate change. Also included is a list of responses to this public letter including policy statements from President Bush and Vice-President Cheney, showing a concern for the energy issues facing our nation and the world. Hopefully this concern will lead to administrative action.

- **National Renewable Energy Laboratory**[15]

  This is a government agency with the honest mission of educating the public and leading us to a sustainable future. On their home page they specifically state that their "research is paving the way to the hydrogen economy." Perhaps this is a government agency that is guiding our decision makers to a future less dependent on fossil fuels. If they are, where is their input when legislative votes are called regarding energy conservation, permitting cars to be considered as trucks (SUV's), or improving fuel mileage standards? It seems like either nobody's listening or they serve a cross-purpose to delude the public into believing all is OK, and our government is watching out for us. With less than 1% of the U.S. energy supply coming from renewable fuels (other than hydro), we are not making progress nearly fast enough to prepare for the coming fossil fuel crisis.

Many additional websites, links, and references provide a variety of energy messages. Following is a partial list of those I have used while researching this book. These are in addition to, or repeat specific cited sources in other chapters. The most comprehensive and pertinent references are listed first:

www.hubbertpeak.com   The basic worldwide site concerning oil depletion.

www.oilcrisis.com   The same site as hubbertpeak.com

www.peakoil.net   The home site for ASPO (The Association for the Study of Peak Oil and Gas). This is the best source for world energy information.

www.asponews.org   The newsletter for ASPO is updated monthly.

www.apolloalliance.org   This is a very aggressive new movement to encourage the public to take control of America's energy future. This website maybe a key to coordination and identification of millions of new related jobs in the critical available time frame facing us.

www.hubbert.mines.edu   This website is prepared by the M. King Hubbert Center of the Colorado School of Mines in Golden, Colorado. The statistics and interpretation are prepared by U.S. geological experts.

www.greatchange.org   An excellent site with an interjection of humor into a very serious subject.

www.after-oil.co.uk   This is the site for the Busby Report referred to later in this book.

www.dieoff.com   Another wonderfully diverse and informative source of related information and references.

www.oilcrash.com   A very comprehensive site originating in New Zealand with many links, books, and essays. People the world over are really trying to be heard.

www.postcarbon.org   Founded by environmental philosopher, Julian Darley. Read "when markets fail-America leaps off the gas cliff without a parachute."

www.directglobalpower.com   Photovoltaic market development.

www.seia.org Solar Energy Industries Association
www.awea.org American Wind Energy Association

The remaining sites are of a more general nature but do cross reference to specific energy issues:

www.forbes.com/energy A good reference for current energy related issues. For instance, see "Rage for SUV's fuels oil import surge." (Dan Ackman, 5/5/03)

www.climatesolutions.org Encourages political and popular support for clean energy and action about global warming.

www.earthfuture.com The name speaks for itself.

www.earthisland.org Another attempt to reach the public.

www.renewables.com Solar power information plus a significant foray into sustainable agriculture and an electric tractor.

www.solarsupply.com This and the next two sites are excellent sources for renewable energy related products and technology.

www.globalissues.co.uk This and the next site give similar messages from England.

www.goinggreen.co.uk

www.simmonsco-intl.com/energyindustry Matthew R. Simmons, the chairman of an international investment company, has been a key advisor to the Bush administration, yet his dire warnings do not seem to receive appropriate attention. You can download his lectures on depletion from www.peakoil.net.

www.syncrude.com Canadian tar sand issues from the optimistic industry viewpoint.

www.egroups.com/science/energy All energy related subjects.

www.oilanalytics.org The alternate site for the Center for Energy and Environmental Studies (CEES).[14]

www.ucsusa.org The home site for the Union for Concerned Scientists.

www.populationconnection.org Focuses on the critical issues of population, which are directly related to energy.

www.nrdc.org (National Resources Defense Council) Energy is only one of many related issues but this is one non-profit that focuses on fuel consumption.

www.nrglink.com An excellent, reasonably priced weekly electronic subscription covering timely energy issues.

www.rmi.org (Rocky Mountain Institute) A strong case for energy efficiency as well as hydrogen and Amory Lovins' hypercar.

www.inri.us Independent Natural Resources Inc. Developer of the "Seadog" wave pump.

www.growbiointensive.org This and the next site teach microagriculture solutions

www.earthship.org

www.copvia.com See "From the Wilderness" published by Michael Ruppert, **www.newrules.org** Advocating a carbohydrate economy

www.pvenergy.com by Paul Maycock, industry consultant and editor of "Photovoltaic News."

www.jjbenergy.com by John Berger, environmental author and consultant

www.ieer.org The Institute for Energy and Environmental Research

www.sustainableusa.org Another attempt to send a message to the public.

www.citizen.org Read about the critical mass energy project.

www.soros.org by philanthropist, George Soros. Encouraging transparency of issues needing public knowledge.

www.energyconservency.org The name speaks for itself.

www.zapworld.com Zero Air Pollution vehicles (all electric) are available in all forms.

www.attra.org The Sustainable Agriculture information service. Does not directly warn of fossil fuel depletion, otherwise, good concepts.

www.aceee.org American Council for an Energy Efficient Economy.

www.cera.com An excellent site for the Cambridge Energy Research Associates headed by Daniel Yergen, author of *The Prize*.

www.evt.com Pertaining to electric vehicles technologies.

www.freerepublic.com   A conservative news site that sometimes explores the news and mysteries of energy.

www.wri.org   The site for The World Resources Institute. Another attempt to reach the public regarding sustainability and climate change.

www.cleanenergystates.org   The site for CESA (Clean Energy States Alliance). At least 12 states joining together to commit to energy related activity that is not being addressed nationally.

www.api.org   (American Petroleum Institute) This site is a typically feel good industry source seemingly more concerned with perpetuating the habit of American culture to consume more deny the message, and ignore the big picture of depletion.

www.whitehouse.gov/energy   The official administrative response alluding to much concern about energy.

There are many other cross links and reference sites, which relate to the crisis at our doorstep but all are limited to internet users and not the general public which is more influenced by mass media.

We are not going to make it to an acceptable civilized future if the public does not hear the story of depletion of finite fossil fuels and plan for an acceptable future lifestyle without plentiful energy.

I repeat again, energy depletion is certain to be the greatest crisis ever to face civilization. Yet, the message is hidden or lost in a blitz of bland media coverage supported by hyperadvertising of high-energy products. Our elected leaders either don't understand or are reluctant to address the subject of energy. Unless we act quickly, we will be fossil fuel bankrupt in another 35 years with very little left for our children. There will be no possibility for a renaissance of an energy intensive civilization. The earth's original endowment of fossil energy will be gone. If you question this statement, investigate the references. I contend the more you research the subject the more concerned you will become.

chapter 4

A Model for an
Energy Sustainable Future

The summary table on page 35 shows 86% of U.S. (and world) energy coming from non-renewable fossil fuels. This is akin to spending 100 dollars with 86 dollars coming from savings and 14 dollars from income. Obviously we're not living within our means. We may continue for a few more years, but there will be little left for the children of today.

The only hope for a future for modern civilization is a fourteen dollar budget for the fourteen dollar income. Once we define that model, we need to construct a plan (or bridge) to get there. In addition to these two daunting tasks is the fact that Americans are sharing this singular bank account with the rest of the world. Other countries, like Germany and Japan, are beginning to plan for the depletion of fossil fuels. The U.S. is lagging behind because of a poorly informed public.

Americans are consuming 25% of the world's energy with only 5% of the population. We have the greatest adjustments to make.

Natives on a remote island will have far fewer problems in a post-fossil fuel era (unless climate change from fossil fuels disrupts their balance with nature). Their lifestyle and consumption has changed little from their predecessors. The higher we are on the Hubbert's Peak of energy consumption, the farther we have to descend.

There are a number of well-established, non-fossil energy sources that make up the remaining 14% of our energy consumption. All, except nuclear, can be considered renewable and therefore a basis for an energy sustainable society. The quantitative contributions from each source, both at the present and proposed for the future, are shown in Chapter 5, pages 65 and 66.

Hydroelectric - a well-accepted source of energy for years but most favorable sites have already been used for decades and water flow is unpredictable.

Solar - both photovoltaic and nonelectric (active or passive) - the technology is well established but requires huge financial investments and energy input to scale up to the levels we will need.

Wind - rapidly expanding in many parts of the world but limited to favorable sites. Both solar and wind are sporadic sources of energy which require either energy input for backup or substantial provision for storage.

Bio-energy - only if we live within a "bio-budget" and not divert biomass that should be used for food. Bio-energy production also has to be in equilibrium with other natural resources and fertile soil maintenance.

Tidal, Geothermal, etc. - these will continue as localized sources but not in magnitude large enough to affect the overall numbers.

Muscle - The work that was done by direct human and draft labor sufficed until the last few centuries, but as explained in Chapter 2, it is so minute compared to what we use now with fossil or renewable sources that it will not be included in the following quantitative design. The intent is to define a future high technology society without returning to back breaking drudgery.

Nuclear falls into a contentious zone. It is not a fossil fuel, but like fossil fuels, it is not sustainable because of finite uranium availability. The uranium ore also requires large quantities of fossil fuel for extraction and shipment. The dangerous record and stigma of nuclear health hazards is well documented. For the remainder of this book, I will continue to use nuclear power at the present level through the Five Percent plan (as explained in Chapter 5) and into a truly energy sustainable society. This is necessary because:

1. We will need all the energy we can find to help us bridge the gap to true sustainability.
2. Nuclear energy production will not be expanded. Instead existing facilities will be allowed to run their course.
3. It is a substantial part of energy supply in other parts of the world, and when used properly is gaining some respect.
4. The problems of waste disposal and public perception appear to be improving as remaining facilities are carefully controlled. This is only an opinion. At least things do not seem to be getting worse in the mature years of this energy source.
5. Improvements in technology may allow us to continue using some forms of nuclear energy beyond the demise of fossil fuels. We should continue its use and development, but on a very guarded basis.

With only the energy available from these non-fossil sources, it is paramount for survival that we design a new, low-energy lifestyle. Then we must plan on how to get to this new state with the remaining fossil energy we have left in the bank before it is frivolously used. If we lose this opportunity to change now, our chances for a modern civilization will be lost forever.

A vision of a modern lifestyle using non-fossil energy, rather than reverting to a hunter/gatherer/agricultural subsistence and without significant breakthroughs like fusion energy is as follows:

1. Continue using centralized generating systems and utility grids we have now. This will allow a gradual transition to the new fossil fuel free system by blending together the present era with the future.
2. Start building decentralized (distributed) solar energy systems (both electrical and heating) in all new and existing

47

homes. Every home becomes an independent power plant. We have the technology now; our ancestors did not.

3. Drastically downscale all travel and movement of goods with the ultimate goal of electric mass transportation. Small electric vehicles will provide for individual needs. It's either that, ride the bike, walk, or stay home.

4. Save precious remaining fossil fuels for agricultural, military, municipal fuel, important mass transportation, and emergency uses. If we start immediately to conserve these fuels, we might buy enough time to invent new high-energy sources while we still have the infrastructure of a functioning society. At least we could save enough fossil energy to ration over an additional hundred years. (See Chapter 5, "The Five Percent Plan.")

5. Our remaining finite supply of fossil fuels must also be available to make the transition to sustainability. This makes possible the infrastructure we need to make solar cells, windmill blades, and continued research and development of new energy sources.

Before describing the details of the plan, let me reiterate, I am an engineer faced with a problem and proposing a solution. If you question or disagree with the premises and conclusions, verify the presented facts. Search for other opinions just as you would if faced with major surgery. Remember, we, collectively, have an undeniable terminal illness, and the only hope is to do something drastic, soon, before it's too late. I am only a messenger presenting well-documented data and logical conclusions.

There are three basic parts in the proposed future, sustainable model:

1. THE PRIVATE RESIDENCE (PR)

Let's start with the private home. This decentralized (distributed) energy source will have to supply most of the energy for both the dwelling and a personal transportation vehicle (PTV) or multipurpose electric utility vehicle (EUV).

Each home becomes a small free enterprise electricity producer of about 4 kw peak power capacity. This requires 40 square meters (435 square feet or a typical roof side) of photovoltaic panels. The cost in 2003 dollars would be about $20,000, enough for a basic 2-car garage. At this cost, the 87 billion dollars just appropriated for Iraq would take care of 4½ million homes. Half of this capacity (2 kw) would suffice for adequate requirements in parts of the country with more sunlight. By cooperating with a utility interactive (UI) grid where power can flow, to or from the central distribution facility (CDF), many homes smooth the storage for others, interconnect with centralized energy sources, and reduce the need for batteries. Residential power bought or sold from the centralized grid would be metered and priced high enough to encourage conservation and maximize individual output.

Typical energy usage from a 4 kw peak power system (2 kw in the sunny southwest) would yield about 400 kwh per month (4800 kwh/yr) even in the cloudy northeast. This 400 kwh per month budget could allow a typical household consumption budget as follows:

200kwh	for personal transportation (PTV) or multipurpose vehicle (EUV) used for both transportation and home agriculture
85kwh	hot water heating (good for one shower or bath every 2 days)
15kwh	high efficiency (12ft.^{3}) full-size refrigerator
30kwh	(2) small cooking burners
8kwh	(1) well insulated oven
12kwh	TV, computer, and communications
8kwh	washing machine
12kwh	lighting
12kwh	water pump
12kwh	miscellaneous power tools and efficiency losses
6kwh	toaster and vacuum
400kwh	Total/month

In June 1997, the Clinton administration proposed the Million Solar Homes Initiative. Now, six years later, little has happened, and time is running out.

With this proposed system on 40 million homes (approximately all the private residences in the U.S. today), the equivalent fossil fuel power plant production, at 35% efficiency would only be 0.3 EBBO. (See appendix 1 for detailed calculations.) This proposed individual residence (PR) electrical energy plan supplies far less than our present wasteful energy consumption, but for Third World societies or our grandparents, such energy availability and consumption would be positively extravagant.

Remember, this decentralized distributed energy plan only supplies our electrical needs for personal transportation (and/or micro-farming), a small bit of hot water for dish washing and about 30 quick showers, and minimal other residential requirements. All of the home heating and most hot water requirements would have to come from active or passive (thermal) solar heating, well-established technology used today throughout the world. All new homes should be built on a smaller scale and with maximum thermal efficiency. Existing homes could be retrofitted and reconfigured so the actual living area reduces to a warm core part of the home for the cold winter months. Assuming the non-photovoltaic solar heating installed in each of the 40 million homes for domestic hot water and some domestic heating is equal to the photovoltaic energy, the total would double the decentralized supply output to 0.6 EBBO annually. (0.3 EBBO photovoltaic and 0.3 EBBO thermal)

This total amount of photovoltaic electric, active, and passive solar energy generated from 40 million residences (0.6 EBBO) is the same order of magnitude as the extra fossil fuel consumed in one year driving SUV's (light trucks) instead of commonly available 35 mpg cars (a difference of 0.44 EBBO).

The battery storage for each personal residence (PR) would depend on individual situations and the dependability of the inter-tied central distribution facility (CDF). Also, the onboard batteries in the personal transportation or electric utility vehicle could supplement the stationary battery pack in each home. As miniscule as it may seem, each of the 800 kwh/month residential systems (400 kwh photovoltaic plus 400 kwh passive) is equivalent to the human energy of 67 people working for one month of forty hour weeks at 75 watts, without the need for food or shelter.

The other renewable fuel for domestic heating in colder climates is the old bio-energy standby, wood. We can only use this sparingly as it is very polluting, and it would take at least an acre of woodlot to continuously provide a cord of wood every year to heat a small, efficient home. The old Yankee rule of thumb is five acres of woodlot for yearly sustainable heating a typical, drafty farmhouse.

An additional intriguing use of PR electricity production could be for a personal agricultural tractor. In the spring and summer an excess of solar or photovoltaic energy from each home could be used to power a small tractor of between 5 and 10-horse power. A number of attachments could be used such as a sickle bar mower, rotary tiller, traditional plow, or wagon. It could also be used to power an electric chain saw or other portable tools. It is also possible that the personal agricultural tractor function could be combined with the personal transportation vehicle into one electric utility vehicle (EUV). In direct sunlight, the proposed residential photovoltaic array could almost supply the tractor with full power on a one to one time basis with incoming solar energy especially if an additional photovoltaic canopy is mounted on the electric vehicle.

If we spend time growing food instead of mowing lawns, the number one crop in the U.S. with 32 million acres, we will be much less dependent on centralized agriculture and food distribution. Home food production will have to become a way of life.

---

2. THE CENTRALIZED DISTRIBUTION FACILITY (CDF)

The central control for the new energy system will be a distribution facility located at or near an existing public utility plant. The purpose of the CDF is to mix all energy inputs and outputs for a surrounding region and smooth the demand and supply so net energy flow is neutral. This would minimize the need for batteries in each PR. Publicly owned CDFs would also include large scale photovoltaic production equal to the total residential (distributed) output of 0.6 EBBO bringing the total U.S. solar contribution by 2050 to 1.2 EBBO/yr. Extensive wind energy farms could supply the CDF with another 0.3 EBBO/yr. This is twice the wind energy projected by the Energy Information Agency (EIA) in their high renewable National Energy Modeling System (NEMS) for the year 2025. The total electricity produced by renewable solar and wind would be 0.6 (CDF) plus 0.3 (PR), plus 0.3 (wind), or 1.2 EBBO/yr. This is just 20% of our 2001 electrical usage of 5.96 EBBO/yr.

The large financial investment for each CDF would come from a stockholder corporation. The energy flow would be closely controlled and supplemented in a manner compatible with government mandates considering the availability of diminishing fossil fuels. Close monitoring and regulation will be required to control the pace at which contemporary fossil fuels are rationed and phased out. We need a national guidance for this huge task at hand. Governmental regulation must have the long-term interests of our society as top priority. Short-term market place interests and profits will only put us back on the track we are now, and we'll never make it to the future.

Our only hope is for an informed constituency,
demanding equitable laws and changes for everyone.
This is a lot to ask, but it must happen.

---

3. THE PERSONAL TRANSPORTATION VEHICLE (PTV) AND THE ELECTRIC UTILITY VEHICLE (EUV)

Automobiles and airplanes are the highly visible symbols of the fossil energy age. Only liquid hydrocarbon fuels can provide the necessary high energy to low weight and volume ratios required for rapid personal movement. A centralized coal plant, nuclear, or hydro cannot provide the lightweight energy package we need to carry with us on a trip. Extension cords don't go very far, and it takes fifty times more weight in lead-acid batteries to provide the same energy storage as liquid fossil fuels. Arguably, synthetic fuels or steam energy could be made from coal, shale oil, tar sands, or biomass. These would be a temporary answer only until we totally run out of these dirty fuels or deplete our forests and croplands. Biomass energy should be reserved for personal energy requirements (food), top soil maintenence, and minimal wood heating.

The only other known way to concentrate enough energy for rapid personal transportation is to use renewable energy sources to make pure hydrogen from the electrolysis of water. This liquid hydrogen would have to be carried on board at very high pressure or in a matrix of exotic metal hydrides. Either way would require a very large container or extremely thick walls. As needed, the hydrogen could be converted to electricity in a complicated fuel cell or be used as an internal combustion fuel. As stated earlier, billions of dollars have already been spent on this technology with little commercial success to date. The best possible place for hydrogen in a realistic distributed energy model may be as a temporary energy storage system at the CDF. Excess electricity flowing into the CDF could be converted by electrolysis to hydrogen. The short-term stored energy could then be converted back to electricity during periods when demands exceed supply. The popular subject of hydrogen is discussed further in other chapters.

At this time, there does not appear to be any reasonable, established technology to satisfy the energy requirements for high speed personal transportation in a non-fossil fuel society without rapid depletion of biomass.

Mass transit could revert to rail systems with electricity coming from the CDF. This would be similar to today's subways and the electric trolleys of the early 20th century. Water travel will have to go back to sail power possibly augmented by solar electricity. We will have to stop moving ourselves and use our new communication technologies for conveyance of messages and visual images. Shipment of goods will also have to be reduced to an absolute minimum.

As fossil fuels become more scarce, personal transportation (other than on a domestic animal) will revert to walking, bicycles, or possibly a personal transportation vehicle (PTV), which is battery powered from energy generated from the CDF or the private residence (PR). This proposal may at first seem unrealistic, but the technology is available in golf carts and electric vehicles already on the market. There have been many attempts to market electric personal vehicles, but commercial success so far has been limited because of overwhelming competition from fossil fuels (see www.zapworld.com).

A typical personal transportation vehicle (PTV) with the following specifications can be built with today's technology:

Gross weight	1000 pounds
Dry vehicle weight	350 pounds (fiberglass and aluminum)
Batteries	450 pounds (approx. 8kwh capacity deep cycle)
1 passenger and load	200 pounds (not very much! There could be room for a 2nd passenger and possibly a child.)
Max continuous power	5 kw. Typical of GE model D29EO DC golf cart motor (65 lbs.)
Voltage	48v DC
Max current	78 amps
Coefficient of drag (C_D)	less than 0.3 (Readily achievable using a shaped fiberglass body.)
Frontal area (A)	less than 12ft^2
Top speed	over 50 mph. (No problem, could reach 60 mph on the level.)
	Hill climbing and acceleration will be adequate and will depend on the type of transmission and motor controller used.
Range (with regenerative braking and efficient wheel hub motors)	1½ hours or up to about 60 miles.

54

This range might be stretched to above two hours to 80 miles at 40 mph since it takes much less force to push the vehicle at slower speeds. The force to overcome wind resistance is proportional to speed squared. One half the speed takes one-fourth the force and energy. That's why we will have to move much more slowly in the future as explained in Chapter 2.

An alternative to a light-weight PTV could be an electric utility vehicle (EUV) that would not only provide tractor power for micro-farming but could double as a 25 mph PTV on the road. This dual purpose vehicle might have the following design and performance specifications:

Gross weight	2100 lbs.
Dry vehicle weight	1400 lbs.
Batteries	450 lbs. (approx. 8 kwh capacity deep cycle) plus another 500 lbs. on a trailer
Max. continuous power	11 kw (typical of advanced X91-4003 model, 60 lbs.)
Voltage	72 to 96 VDC
Max. current	115 amps continuous
Top speed	25 mph.
Range	50-100 miles (with photovoltaic canopy or approximately one hour of land plowing, the toughest agricultural requirement)

This EUV would be similar in size to a 1950's vintage Farmall Cub. By adding 100 square feet of photovoltaic canopy (50 sq.ft. above the tractor and an equal amount above a trailer) an additional 900 watts (1.2 Hp) could be realized in direct sunlight. This would be enough to propel the EUV-trailer combination up to 20 mph with no battery discharge on a sunny day. It's conceivable that 100 miles could be covered on a bright summer day with sophisticated design and no battery recharging from an external source. The electric EUV concept makes sense because extra battery weight is beneficial for traction and there is more sunlight in the spring and summer months. An example of such a vehicle has been built by the author and is shown on the back cover.

These proposed concepts for transportation and farming sound feeble and should not be compared to 150 Hp cars and 50 Hp tractors but they offer the only chance to continue a semblance of a modern civilization. In the long-term, large scale commercial farming will eventually have to revert to a percentage use of oxen, horses, and mules because the manure (also called black gold at one time) is essential to maintain soil productivity. A farmer cannot continue to export energy in the form of food without returning to the land what is removed. Commercial fertilizer and inexpensive fossil fuels will no longer be available. Eventually, population will have to significantly decline and relocate back to many small farms. A comprehensive plan for energy reduction as proposed in Chapter 5 is the only way we can make it in the future.

The concept of a solar and wind powered society is not new. Several European countries have committed to substantial wind energy contribution to electrical needs by 2020. Dr. Hermann Scheer is a member of parliament for the German government and winner of several prizes for his work on renewable energy. His comprehensive book on the subject is titled, *The Solar Economy, Renewable energy for a Sustainable Future*[1] and is now available in English translation. In addition to direct solar and wind, Dr. Scheer relies heavily on biomass as a major substitute for fossil energy. Unfortunately, he does not quantitatively explain the sources of energy to produce the biomass, the loss of food by diverting bioenergy to biofuel, and the problems of water and soil depletion.

In the final fossil fuel free civilization, all energy will have to come from concurrent solar radiation. This must even include the energy to reproduce the hardware necessary for long-term sustainability. The head start we have now, due to the carry over of remaining fossil energy, will eventually be used up. Our descendents will not only have to obtain renewable, non-fossil energy for food and all other needs, they will also have to rely on incoming solar power to manufacture new solar cells, batteries, copper wire, structural steel, aluminum, and on and on.

This challenge may seem overwhelming and barely conceivable, but it can be done in theory. For instance, a photovoltaic solar system that could last 50 years requires only one or two years of returned energy for replacement. The following table quantifies the weight of various materials that can be raised to melting temperature (specific heat) and then melted (heat of fusion) with just one 4 kw (the size proposed for each residence) photovoltaic system providing 4800 kwh (16 million BTU) per year at 50% efficiency for one year:

Lead	264,000 pounds (enough for about 4,000 batteries)
Copper	29,304 pounds (enough for 400 electric cars, tractors, or homes)
Steel	22,408 pounds (enough for 200 vehicles or 20 transmission towers)
Aluminum	23,120 pounds (a substitute for steel)
Glass	5,200 pounds (as needed)

Obviously this type of energy usage and capital investment would be done at centralized facilities. Also, transportation and the energy for ore extraction will have to be provided by centralized solar and hydro using batteries or hydrogen for storage.

Eventually, even the ore for each material will become so depleted that all subsequent material requirements will have to come from recycling. By that time, we will experience population reduction and drift slowly backwards from any semblance of an industrialized modern civilization. It may be that the 200-year fossil fuel consumption curve is just a small blip in a much larger ten to twenty thousand year finite metal resource epoch that spans the copper and iron ages of civilization.

Taking this line of reasoning further, it could be argued that it is impossible for an advanced civilization to exist anywhere in the universe for longer than a few thousand years. The very unique circumstances required to concentrate metals and energy on a singular planet cannot provide enough resources to last longer than a few years in the cosmological time frame. The time frame for space travel evolution may, in reality, be impossible.

This is not a unique concept (see *The Olduvai Theory: Sliding towards a Post-Industrial Stone Age*[2]). This philosophy of time-limited resources may answer some very perplexing questions:

Are we alone in the universe?

How did we get to the standard of living we enjoy in our modern industrialized world?

What will be the future of our species?

What life on earth will our immediate and long-term descendants experience?

Can we control our destiny?

What will be the time frame for our civilization?

How does our species fit into the long-term picture of biological evolution?

Would it be better for fewer people to enjoy a longer industrial age or more people to shorten it?

Is there a religious interpretation for the depletion of finite resources, both long-term for metals and short-term for fuels?

Finally, it is worth noting that there are two excellent contemporary and contrasting examples of post fossil fuel industrialized societies. When Russian oil exports to North Korea and Cuba ceased, following the collapse of the Soviet Union, both countries were faced with a serious life-threatening shortfall of energy. North Korea has done little but experience infrastructure collapse and starvation. Cuba, on the other hand, has made an about-face to decentralized microagriculture and has become a model of agricultural reform in the developing world. For instance, urban gardens alone grow half the produce consumed in Havana and 215 grams (about one half pound) of vegetables per day per person for the entire population. For in-depth discussion see "Drawing Lessons from Experience: The Agricultural Crisis in North Korea and Cuba" by Dale Allen Pfeiffer.[3]

chapter 5

The Five Percent Plan
to Energy Sustainability

After 100 years of plentiful energy, we find ourselves perched precariously on top of "Hubbert's Peak." In Chapter 4, we envisioned a fossil fuel free lifestyle and a future with much lower energy. The challenge for our high-flying society is how to get there before we completely run out of the temporary, high energy support system on which we've built our present levels of population and consumption. This may not be the best scenario because it infers that all we have to do is coast back down to a sustainable future. In reality, we'll need all the fossil energy we have to make the transition and still leave a small amount left for absolute necessities.

An example of our present plight might be a team of astronauts on the moon. From this precarious position, they must get back to a basic sustainable environment before their artificial, finite life support system runs out. If their previously stored energy supply is depleted, they will never make it.

Like astronauts or occupants of a life boat, we must share the challenges and resource rationing of the return trip as provisions become scarce. It seems preposterous that intelligent, informed human beings resist working

> together to survive, but that's exactly what is beginning
> to happen as we squabble like typical animals over
> dwindling resources.[1,2,3]

Many reputable scholars and scientists have been warning for
years of the pending collapse of our high-energy civilization.
How much time we have left to design and cross the bridge is not
exactly clear, but it most certainly depends on how soon we get
started. There appear to be two positions on the subject. One
group predicts an inevitable decline of high energy civilization in
the next 10 to 20 years. Referenced websites in Chapter 3 link to
many highly qualified and concerned authors. Their books and
papers have titles like, *The Olduvai Theory, Sliding towards a Post-
Industrial Stone Age* by Richard C. Duncan (the Olduvai Gorge is
a well know prehistoric site in Africa where humans originated),[4]
Energy and Human Evolution by Dr. David Price,[5] and the recently issued, *The Party's Over* by Richard Heinberg,[6] *The Oil
Crash and You*, by Bruce Thompson,[7] and *Oil Depletion in the U.S.
and the World*, by Suppo A. Korpela.[8]

The second, happy camp seems to be dominated by government supported agencies and related research groups. Imbedded
in this second group are shadows of the business world and world
energy corporations. Although some of these companies, such as
British Petroleum and Shell, put out comprehensive websites de-
lineating fossil fuel reserves and consumption rates, none seem to
want to send a clear message of hard times ahead. I think of these
as "feel good" websites versus the "gloom and doom" messages
of the first group. It is difficult to understand the different approaches to this subject because the above mentioned oil companies do agree, quantitatively, with the "gloom and doom"
prophets of the first group, but there has been a tradition among
economists and oil people that since the reserve to production
ratio (R/P) of oil, natural gas, or coal remains somewhat constant
that all is okay. Short-term interests and profits are satisfied.
This is misleading. A better indicator of future production is the
ratio of new discoveries to present consumption. This number
has been declining for years, and we are now using oil at a rate
four times higher than we are finding it.

To design the path (bridge) to sustainability, I will continue to use equivalent billion barrels of oil (EBBO) as the fundamental unit of consumption for all finite fossil fuels as well as the nuclear and renewable energy sources on which we will have to depend. Natural gas is our next favorite fuel, and these reserves are not much better than oil. As we've seen, the world's oil production is near its peak in 2003. Natural gas is definitely becoming harder to find and production will fall soon after oil. There are more sources of coal, but its use is very environmentally destructive. It also takes considerable fossil fuel energy to remove it from the earth. It has been projected that by the year 2040, it will take twice as much energy to mine and process coal than the coal can provide.[9]

To design the plan to sustainability, we will consider natural gas and coal to have the same finite reserve life as oil. As an engineer, I've learned to design on the conservative side. Engineers like to talk in terms of safety factors to allow for unexpected pitfalls and fuzzy numbers. For a subject as serious as the future of modern civilization, it seems prudent to stack the deck as much as possible in our favor.

In Chapter 3, pages 35 and 37, I summarize annual U.S. energy consumption to date, in terms of equivalent billion barrels of oil (EBBO) used each year. The path to the future, as described in Chapter 4, starts with this same bell shaped probability curve. I focus on U.S. consumption for a number of reasons:

- Other countries such as Germany, Denmark, and Japan are already ahead of the U.S. in their quest for sustainability. Also, some countries use different mixes of energy to make up their total consumption.

- We live in a global economy using global resources. The U.S. uses far more total energy as well as twice the energy per capita than any other developed country. We are the bad guys using more than our share. We have the largest correction to make. The world looks to the U.S. for leadership, but they're not

The End of Fossil Energy

Total U.S. Energy Consumption Showing the Five Percent Plan to Energy Sustainability

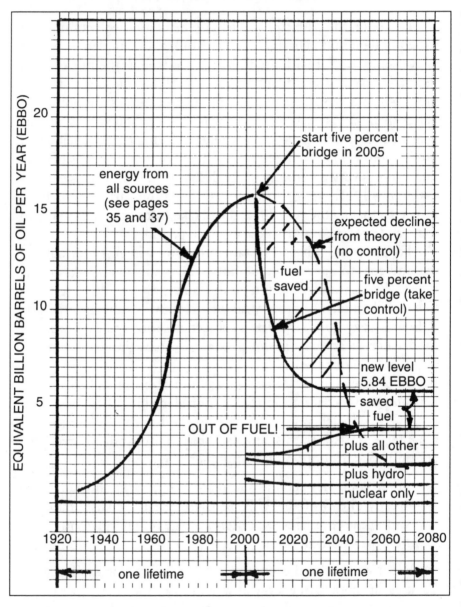

62

seeing it in terms of energy conservation and rapid deployment of renewable energy. Even the utopian fossil fuel, free energy model envisioned in Chapter 4 provides more energy for the U.S. than the undeveloped Third World uses today and considerably more than our great grandparents had without fossil fuels.

- If we take the initiative in this endeavor, the world will think better of us than our reputation for laying claim to remaining reserves and conspicuously consuming the world's resources.

The solid line on the right side of the preceding curve is our direction following the controlled Five Percent Plan. The broken line is the expected decline in consumption if we do nothing. To reach sustainability hinges on four significant commitments. Without all four, all bets are off. We can only expect to slide into chaos, anarchy, and starvation.

1. THE FIVE PERCENT PLAN (BRIDGE)

The curtailment of fossil fuel consumption is the focal point of the second half of this book. We must start immediately to reduce our oil, natural gas, and coal consumption by at least five percent per year. This will be fairly easy for us because of today's excessive waste. In addition we should realize improvements in our overall well-being. I will expand on the details of the changes we have to make in Chapter 6. For our and our children's future, we need to start on the Five Percent Plan now. A close look at the numbers shows why this is true. (The quantitative annual reduction for the Five Percent Plan is summarized in Appendix 4.)

2. NEGATIVE POPULATION GROWTH (NPG)

We cannot continue to grow in population. As we run short of fossil fuels, especially for producing nitrogen fertilizer and the energy intensive agriculture needed to grow and distribute food, we will not be able to feed any more people or even the numbers we have now. It takes about one EBBO of energy just to feed the current U.S. population of 280 million people. We must begin to move toward negative population growth. The average number of children per couple must be less than 1.5 if long-term population is to peak and begin to decline. More children consume more than a fair share of resources. Quality of life, per capita energy, and food supply all suffer accordingly. This is a tough subject, but if we don't take control of the numbers, simple mathematics will be our demise. The majority of the world suffers today from the simple problem of overpopulation. There are too many hungry bodies and not enough food. This is occurring even with an overflow of energy, which filters its way into the Third World but will not be there in the future. Hard times are coming because we did not stop multiplying when resources were plentiful. Ultimately, our population will eventually have to decrease to about a 25% level, proportional to our decreased energy usage. The low energy world of the future will not be able to provide for all of the children born today.

3. GO SOLAR

The proposed sustainable energy plan hinges on a total commitment to solar electricity and heating, especially on a residential basis. The plan is outlined in Chapter 4, "A Model for an Energy Sustainable Future." This plan requires 40 million individual residences (about one for every seven people of today's 280 million U.S. population) to have solar systems by 2050. Chapter 4 explains how and why decentralized solar energy sources will also have to provide energy for most personal transportation as well as substantial local and private food production.

Each of the 40 million residences will produce an average of 4800 kwh per year of electricity and an equal amount of solar heating. This decentralized residential energy capacity combined with an equal amount from centralized solar electricity power plants will provide us with the equivalent of 1.2 billion barrels of oil (EBBO) per year. (See Appendix 1 for the math.)

4. STAY PUT

The short fossil fuel age provides the energy to make possible the excessive distances we travel today. This can be seen in the work equals force times distance equation (Energy = Work = Force x

Distance). All frivolous movement of people and things will soon end. As stated earlier, any speed above 20 mph begins to encounter wind resistance as a major factor Most of the energy of today's travel is expended to overcome the force required to churn and heat surrounding air when we exceed 20 mph.

Drastically reduced travel and speed are not easy pills to swallow, but we have no choice. The math and dwindling high-energy resources will make these changes inevitable. If we control the coming change, we will still have a minimal amount of fossil fuel left for national security, municipal needs, and emergency travel. Life won't be that bad, our great grandparents survived without moving too fast, got good exercise, and met their neighbors.

The following table starts with the present U.S. energy consumption as shown in Chapter 3. These numbers are then projected forward to what they should be by 2050.

(All units are EBBO)	Present U.S. Total Consumption (2001)	Future Energy Consumption (2050)
Finite fossil fuels	13.28 (oil 6.05, natural gas 3.69 coal 3.55)	2.0 from 200 EBBO saved and spread over 100 years
Hydroelectric	(0.379/ 2001, 0.622/1996 with better flow)	0.7 all possible sites maximized, average flow/year
Nuclear	1.20	1.2 we will keep nuclear at the present level but continue to clean up extraction and waste disposal processes (see discussion in Chapter 2)

(continued)

The End of Fossil Energy

(All units are EBBO)	Present U.S. Total Consumption (2001)	Future Energy Consumption (2050)
Wood	0.347	0.3 reduced to sustain resources and because of decreased fossil fuels available for harvesting and transportation
Biowaste	0.088	0.1 continue at present level, but we must have sustainability, including wood, or we'll look like Easter Island
Ethanol	0.023	0 deleted. No fossil fuels will be available to produce ethanol for fuel. All agricultural output required for food. Biofuels are eliminated because production requires more energy than they yield.
Geothermal	0.05	0.05 continue at present level due to rarity of sites
Solar	0.01	1.20 increased more than 100 times as the cornerstone of our future energy needs (see Appendix 1 and Chapter 4)
Wind	0.01	0.30 30 times the present rate. There is considerable additional potential here. The proposed rate is almost twice the NEMS (National Energy Modelling System) high renewable case for 2025.
Total	15.5 (increase to 16.0 in 2003)	5.85

The future energy consumption goal to be reached by 2050 is about 6 EBBO per year. Of this available energy, 36% (2 EBBO) is carried over from fossil fuels conserved using the Five Percent Plan. This reduced level will have to keep us going for another 100 years. If we continue to squander our fossil fuels, as we do now, we will have no chance to bridge the coming crisis.

The lower energy level in 2050 is about one third of our present level of waste and consumption. It would provide a very tolerable lifestyle for our descendents, at least until the middle of the next century. Remember, our ancestors only had muscle power, wood, and coal but far fewer people, no airplanes, and no cars.

If we can buy time for an orderly transition, we will still have the possibility to develop new energy sources such as nuclear fusion. As explained earlier, "the don't worry, be happy" party line is we've always managed to discover or invent new energy sources on a timely basis or devise improved methods to extract more from existing reserves. Experts are now telling us loud and clear, oil and natural gas supplies are significantly declining. Coal appears to be more abundant but in deteriorating sites of accessibility and quality. As explained earlier, more energy will be required for extraction, and the environmental record for coal is worsening.

The curves and numbers in this chapter, show the energy dilemma we're in, especially in the U.S. By reducing our demand on world resources by 200 EBBO over the next 40 years, we can spread these retained fossil fuels over the following 100 years from about 2050 to 2150. This will give us at least one EBBO per year to provide food for our population (see Appendix 2 for the calculation). The other one EBBO saved using The Five Percent Plan would provide for a continuation of centralized governmental infrastructure, national security, pharmaceuticals, lubricants, mass transportation, manufacturing renewable energy equipment (seed energy), all other industry requirements, plastics, etc. In magnitude, the annual conserved fossil fuel energy from the Five Percent Plan (2 EBBO) is almost twice what we expect from 4 kw solar systems installed on 40 million homes plus an equal amount of centralized solar energy production. This may seem futile as we continue to run out of fossil fuel, but increased investment and familiarity with renewables can lead us into a truly sustainable energy future. There is a strong movement happening which shows that this huge change in technology and lifestyle could produce millions of new jobs.[10]

We can deny or argue with the cited references, premises used, and scenarios offered throughout this book but consider the following:

- We are clearly running out of fossil fuels. At our present consumption rate, we will begin a serious downhill slide in the next five to ten years, a time when growing population needs more energy for food and strives for more luxuries. Rising demands and dwindling supplies are on a collision course.

- The U.S. uses about twice as much energy per capita than any other country. We must make the greatest reductions in consumption to reach a new low energy society. If the U.S. takes the lead in downsizing consumption, we could lead the rest of the world in a coordinated effort.

- There are no panaceas or alternatives. It is too late to rely on unproven technology.

- The proposed Five Percent Plan takes us only into the middle of the next century. By then, we will be void of most fossil fuels as well as many other finite resources. Hopefully the extra 100 years gained by conservation will give us the time to plan accordingly.

- By 2150, U.S. population should also decrease to about 70 million people, which is about one fourth of our present 280 million, in order to continue a truly sustainable civilization. The rest of world population will also have to decline at the same rate either by design or the cruel laws of resource depletion.

Our planet will never again be able to support a high
population, industrialized modern civilization at the level
we now enjoy. All of the high-energy fossil fuels, which
took millions of years to accumulate, will have been used
up in a couple of hundred years. There will be little left
for future inhabitants.

- It is understandably difficult for us to notice the transition from increasing to decreasing energy availability. The change from a positive to a negative trend is taking place over several decades and is blurred by many other factors such as price, economics, wars, advertising, and geopolitics. This transition is called an inflection and can be compared to a summer or winter solstice. It is difficult to notice the day by day change in sunlight and weather, but we know it's going to happen and plan accordingly. Winter clothes or bathing suits appear in stores long before the appropriate season arrives. Why don't we plan the same way? We know that overhunting and overfishing are counter productive so we inact laws to prevent depletion. We need to do the same for energy.

- The only hope to maintain the extremely high level of consumption we have now will be to harness a perpetual, clean form of energy like nuclear fusion, which in turn could provide copious amounts of electricity and hydrogen for fuel. The sophistication, energy, and time for this type of research and development cannot be developed in a subsistence society living in huts.

- The only non-fossil energies now are hydro, nuclear fission, bio, solar, and wind. As shown in the earlier table, the energy contributions from these are far less than the energy we use now. Without fossil fuels and nuclear, we could still have 17% of our present energy level. This new lifestyle is only possible if we increase our solar energy 120 times and our wind energy by 30 times in the next 50 years. We better get started.

69

- If there are others who have alternatives to The Five Percent Plan, they should quickly make themselves heard. The proposed plan (or any similar plan for that matter) is very time sensitive and needs to start immediately. If we don't get started, we will lose the time sliver of opportunity. We will have wasted the fossil fuels that our descendants will so desperately need over the next 150 years.

- Note again, as explained in Chapter 3, just the fuel that could be saved by legislated automobile fuel economy (27 mpg) versus light trucks and SUV's (18 mpg) is 0.44 EBBO per year. If we had moved the other way in the 1980's to more efficient vehicles available at the time (35 mpg), we would be saving almost one EBBO per year right now. Gas-guzzlers and frivolous transportation are directly robbing from the future of my and your children.

The difference in fuel consumption, for the same distance traveled, between what we are now using with large cars and light trucks and what we would consume at 60 mpg, is about one fourth all of the energy required for our future model in 2050. Are we the most intelligent species on the earth?

We need to start immediately to reduce our energy consumption by five percent per year. In many ways this action will improve our quality of life. It will also resolve related problems, such as climate change and pollution. The message as summarized in this book must reach a majority of the U.S. public and not stop with you as an individual reader. It's up to everybody to get involved. Civilization cannot survive unless individuals make it happen. Get involved. Pass it on.

chapter 6

Reductions of Energy Usage to Achieve the Five Percent Plan

It's time for a seventh inning stretch. Since starting this project last winter, summer arrived, the lawn is green, and another gallon of gas fueled the plowing of our one fourth acre garden. Hopefully, the Iraq war is behind us and was at least morally justified considering the outgoing regime's horrific human rights record. From an energy perspective, however, some of the incredible amount of fuel used for the three week war and subsequent occupation will ultimately be replenished from the country being liberated. Roman Legions marched using grain (energy) taken from the countries they conquered. Sometime in the next few years there will no longer be enough fossil fuel to support our ability to "shock and awe" and geopolitics will take on new meaning.

Review of Several Contrasting Positions

A three-day international workshop on oil depletion held in Uppsala, Sweden (May 23–25, 2002) was organized by Uppsala University and ASPO (the Association for the Study of Peak Oil and Gas). This meeting and the meeting held in Paris in May of 2003 are covered in great detail on www.peakoil.net. To quote the mission of the first meeting which was attended by experts from all over the world:

> *The Workshop has been organized to address the impact of resource constraints and natural depletion on the global supply of oil, one of Europe's most critical energy sources.*
>
> *The Workshop will examine geological mechanisms of oil generation, the processes of extraction, and the nature of depletion as imposed by reservoir physics.*
>
> *The Workshop will address also the unreliable nature of public data on oil reserves, the record of past oil forecasts, and the misunderstanding of the 'Limits of Growth' message of the 1970's. It will question the ability of conventional economics to handle a rapidly depleting resource, and draw attention to the impact of oil's decline on Europe's economic situation. It will ask why governments are not better informed, and why they fail to make appropriate preparation to ease the impact of the transition from growing to declining oil supply.*

After digesting this report and other considerable input from the web and myriad other sources, I feel even more concerned for the future of humankind. Many put a happy face on the coming crisis by pointing out progress in renewable energy but closer analysis of quantitative details reveals work done so far is absolutely miniscule considering the pace we must attain to reach energy sustainability. For instance, Janet Sawin has written a very informative chapter in *The State of the World 2003*[1] detailing the early solar and wind progress made in Europe and Japan. She also points out the U.S. lags far behind Europe. Like many authors, she does not quantitatively emphasize how insignificant renewable energy progress has been so far compared to the awesome quantity of fossil fuel we now consume and how quickly it is being depleted. When we run out of gas, it's not going to help to find two people instead of one to push the car, even though we've doubled that tiny energy effort. We would need 50 people working in relays to push the car any appreciable distance.

Without belaboring the subject, I would like to compare two contrasting approaches to the subject of energy in the future. First, from a presentation to the British House of Commons by Colin J. Campbell, July 7, 1999[2]:

> *The title of my talk is "The Imminent Peak of World Oil Production." I would like to provide the evidence. It is, of course, a very large subject. There are colossal economic and political consequences. Indeed the very future of our subspecies - Hydrocarbon Man - is at stake.*
>
> *My qualifications for taking up your time are that I have spent the last 45 years studying the subject both directly and indirectly. I have evaluated hundreds of oil projects around the world. I have drilled many dry holes and even made a few discoveries. I have observed the oil industry from many angles, including its senior management. I have published two books and several papers on oil depletion.*
>
> *I think I can summarize the position into a few key points.... We now have a comprehensive understanding of petroleum systems.*
>
> - *It has become relatively easy to identify and map them, once the critical information has been gathered from seismic surveys and excavation bore holes.*
> - *The prolific generation of oil and gas was a very rare event in both time and place in the geological past.*
> - *The world has now been very thoroughly explored with the benefits of this new understanding and the high-resolution seismic surveys. About 90% of the world's oil endowment lies in just 30 major petroleum systems.*
>
> *Looking at the world as a whole, we see this growing deficit, discovery peaked in the 1960's with a 60 Gb surplus, but that has given way to a deficit of almost 20 Gb. We now find one barrel for every four we consume.*

(Note: My comments, remember this was written in 1999. A Gb is a giga barrel, which is the same as one billion barrels.)

73

The general situation seems so obvious. Surely everyone can see it staring them in the face. How can any thinking person not be aware if it? How can governments be oblivious of the realities of discovery and their implications? How is it possible given the critical importance of oil to our entire economy?

It is fashionable to accuse oil companies of conspiracy, but I think the deception has more to do with differing mindset and objectives than conspiracy. Oil companies are in business to make money, not plan the world's future.

I should say something about getting more oil out of the reservoir. You will hear a great deal about that. Now that falling discovery is widely recognized, hopes are pinned on getting more out of what has already been found. I am sorry to say that reports of improved recovery are largely an illusion reflecting the reporting procedure rather than any particular technological improvement.

The bottom line is that there is a rounded one trillion barrels left to produce.

The U.S.–48 is a good example. Discovery peaked in the 1930's and production in 1971, despite ample technology, money, and incentive. In the North Sea, peak discovery around 1980 is now being followed by peak production. It should surprise no one.

One indisputable fact stands out. Discovery peaked 30 years ago. It takes no feat of intellect to conclude that we now face the corresponding peak of production.

Compare the above reality and pessimism with the following excerpts from a talk given by U.S. Energy Secretary Spencer Abraham to the Detroit Economic Club, February 7, 2003:[3]

Back on January 2, 2001, when President Bush asked me to serve as secretary, I recognized as we all do, the importance of energy to our economy and to our way of life, I have to confess, however, that I didn't fully appreciate then just how much my job would relate to this state and to our industries. But the facts are clear - more than two thirds of the 20 million barrels of oil Americans use each day is used for transportation. As a result, a key part of my job is working closely with Detroit and the automotive industry to devise energy solutions for our nation's future.

Last May here at The Club, I noted that the 21st century will bring a huge increase in energy demand. Our analysts foresee a 54 percent increase for electricity ... 54 percent for natural gas ... and 47 percent for oil ... by the year 2025. At the same time we can expect to see similar or even greater increases in energy demand all over the globe.

It is difficult to believe that Campbell and Abraham are talking about the same planet.

Abraham goes on to say about President Bush's 1.7 billion dollar hydrogen initiative:

We believe that the hydrogen economy is our future, so today, the questions we face are how fast this effort should proceed, and whether it will be led by America or by others.

- *First, we must lower the cost of fuel cells by another factor of ten.*
- *Second, we must lower the cost of hydrogen ... virtually all hydrogen manufactured today is produced from natural gas. If successful, fusion could well be the most cost effective source of hydrogen we will ever find.*
- *Third, we must devise new methods to store sufficient amounts of hydrogen fuel aboard a vehicle to provide the consumer with sufficient range.*
- *Fourth, and most critically, we will work to solve the overarching infrastructure challenges I just outlined.*

As a result of this effort, we estimate that by 2020, we could achieve mass-market penetration of hydrogen fuel cell vehicles and the availability of fueling stations nationwide.

The above sounds like five miracles end to end, all by 2020 and nowhere in the EIA's forecast to 2025 is there provision for hydrogen. As a lifelong car enthusiast, mechanical engineer, and career product development manager, I would not put all my 1.7 billion dollars into this basket. All the above research has been going on for years with little to show for it except research grants and fuel for our space program.

Science and math predict that the age of high speed travel will end soon. The required concentrated energy will become increasingly scarce and there are far more important uses for what is left.

Referring to and re-emphasizing the U.S. energy consumption curve, past and future, shown on page 37, note well that the first half of the bell shaped probability curve takes place in one long 80 year lifetime.

On this same bell shaped curve, the second half of total recoverable crude oil also occurs in one lifetime of children being born today. Two lifetimes, that's all, for the energy party. This is a blink of a blink, in the human timeline of world history.

The actions we take today will directly affect our children's survival. We must act now or lose the small window of opportunity to climb down a ladder from this peak we're on. The alternative is to decline into a nation and world of chaos and misery.

If we really love America and our descendents, we must raise a common voice to demand sweeping legislation so all citizens (not just a conscientious few) begin immediately to reduce energy consumption.

THE FIVE PERCENT PLAN
(See Appendix 4 for Summary)

Following are the four major sectors of U.S. energy consumption where we must begin immediately to save energy. The first reductions are easy since we have the highest per capita consumption in the world. We'll be better off as a society and see corresponding improvements in overall health and environment.

1. Transportation
(4.25 EBBO, 28% of total energy consumption)

The age of fast travel will end with the age of fossil energy.

• Big Cars (and trucks) to Smaller Vehicles

The first step (and easiest) of our controlled descent down the Five Percent Plan requires getting out of our gas guzzlers. As pointed out in Chapter 3, the use of light trucks (SUV's) at 18 mpg compared to ordinary cars at 28 mpg is costing us 0.44 EBBO per year. By driving readily available 35 mpg cars, we could save an additional 0.42 EBBO per year for a total of 0.86 EBBO. These two steps alone would take care of our total first year's goal of the Five Percent Plan. I believe a majority of citizens are ready for and believe in this move but are reluctant to do so because of intimidation by oversized vehicles and present low fuel costs. A combination of fuel taxes and rationing would encourage equitable restraint by everyone. If someone were in your garden stealing your food, you'd complain. Someone is stealing your and your children's energy. Raise a voice. Switching from big vehicles to little ones would reduce consumption, improve safety, and not hinder our lifestyle. We need legislation, which encourages a profound change in our thinking. Are you part of the problem or a solution?

• **Drive Less**

The next easy step is to consider if each trip is really necessary. I remember WWII when my parents had gas stamps for 5 gallons per week. That was a time of war and an accepted temporary crisis. What could be more of a permanent crisis than the one we are facing in the next 5 to 10 years? Walking and bicycling instead of driving would make us healthier. Planning multiple trips into one, using public transportation, car-pooling, vacationing closer to home, all could easily be done. By reducing our travel by 50% (and using 35 mpg cars) we could take another giant step towards reducing energy consumption. In the year 2000, 280 million Americans traveled 2,525,000 million (over two trillion) miles in their cars and light trucks (SUV's). By reducing this excessive travel by one half with our new 35 mpg vehicles, we would save another 0.86 EBBO.

This brings us down the ladder to the year 2006 on our controlled Five Percent Bridge. This is easy. We've already saved (0.86 + 0.86) = 1.72 EBBO (11% of 2001 total energy), and we're safer and healthier for it.

We're starting to look like Europeans, little cars, short trips. People around the world are starting to respect us.

The economy has kept busy using still available energy to melt down big cars to build smaller ones and, if priced right, automobile manufacturers could still make a profit. The little cars will keep us going in great style providing we don't increase the population and negate the gains we've made. Little cars will also make it safer for electric cars and hybrids to appear on the road.

• **Alternative Vehicles**

Switching to even more efficient vehicles such as hybrids, small diesels (already popular in Europe today), and electric cars could easily increase our average gas mileage to about 60 mpg. This is well within the reach of today's technology. Who knows, maybe a little hydrogen derived from fossil fuels might be introduced, although the complexity, required infrastructure, and drastically reduced emissions we've already achieved make hydrogen-powered vehicles superfluous and complicated. By going from 35 mpg to 60 mpg and traveling 50% less in our personal cars, we save an additional:

0.86 EBBO used at 35 mpg minus 0.505 EBBO used at 60 mpg = 0.36 EBBO

Our total energy savings is now (0.86 + 0.86 + 0.36) = 2.08 EBBO, or about one half of our 2001 level of the total energy (4.25 EBBO per EIA) used for transportation.

· Diesel Fuel

In 2001, we used 0.934 EBBO for diesel fuel, about one third the energy used for cars and light trucks. We can cut this in half just by slowing down and not shipping stuff from coast to coast. This would give us another 0.47 EBBO. Less interstate transport would encourage a renewal of local commerce and agriculture with a commensurate return to local employment.

I can hear the screams of anguish. "We can't shut down the economy this way." Listen to the laws of science and do the math. If we don't slow down on our terms now, in another ten to twenty years civilization will begin to collapse, and we will spiral out of control with very little fuel left.

· Air Travel

In 2001, jet fuel amounted to 0.6 EBBO. We should start right away to also cut this in half giving us a total for both diesel and jet fuel of 0.77 EBBO.

0.47 EBBO diesel + 0.30 EBBO air = 0.770 EBBO

This brings us to a total energy consumption of 13.15 EBBO per year, the point we should reach in about four years after starting in 2005.

• **Marine**

Of course marine travel, like all other forms of moving people or things over a distance, will also have to decline and use renewable energy. Since this mode of travel is in the commercial sector, the quantitative reductions of energy will have to come from there.

• **Military and National Security**

It's not clear where U.S. government and military energy consumption is shown in the EIA summary. One reference reports 993×10^{12} BTU/year (0.158 EBBO) for the war year 1991.[4] Like all other sectors of consumption, military use must also be significantly reduced in the future. As a functioning nation, our primary concern, other than food and energy, is national security. For this reason, it is critical that we preserve our fossil fuel resources as much as possible. I don't believe even the most optimistic dreamers can envision solar jet planes or hydrogen powered tanks. As the second half of our 200-year fossil fuel era winds down, nations with fossil energy will be the ones that control their security. This is an extremely serious consideration which is underlying much the world's geopolitical unrest.

Do our long-range military planners understand where the fuel for national security is going to come from 50 to 100 years from now? This is another reason it is especially important that we start immediately on our Five Percent per year reduction plan.

Our total U.S. petroleum reserves of 0.7 EBBO in the Louisiana Salt Mines and an estimated 7.0 EBBO (one year's consumption at our present rate) yet untapped resources in the Artic National Wildlife Reserve in Alaska (ANWR) will be far more important for our future survival than for frivolous use today.

• **Recreation**

All unnecessary use of fuel will have to end. A joy ride we enjoy today is future energy lost forever for humanity.

80

Now things are really getting serious. Some favorites that quickly come to mind are:

Internal combustion racing of any kind:

A quick calculation of a single major Nascar race with 50,000 spectators driving, four in a car, 100 miles at 20 mpg plus transporters and 50 race cars shows a fuel consumption of 75,000 gallons of fuel. We should watch bicycle racing instead as the race comes through the villages to the spectators. In the three week Tour de France, close to one fourth of the population will see the race live, many without having to travel by car.

All other spectator functions:

About 95% of the energy cost of automobile racing, is the fuel consumed by spectators. Similar reductions will have to be made in all activities where the mode of travel is other than foot, bicycle or mass transit. How can we enjoy consuming fuel for pleasure when we will need it for future survival? Think about it. We should stay home and watch spectator sports on TV or participate in activities which emphasize human energy.

Other Sports:

There are other very energy intensive sports; for instance, (one of my favorites) alpine skiing which combines personal travel, second homes, or overnight facilities (heated and available), and extensive electricity for snowmaking and lifts.

School Buses and Soccer Moms:

We probably use more energy for school transportation, sports, and related activities than many Third World nations use for everything. School travel will have to rely on public mass transportation, bicycles, or walking. I'm not dreaming this up. We must use less fuel. Our kids must learn what the low energy future holds for them.

RV's, ATV's, Personal Watercraft, etc.:

In light of dwindling and finite fossil fuel resources, all of these activities will have to cease. This is not a personal vendetta. The party's over. (This was written before the book of the exact title appeared on the market.[5]) How can so few take from so many? These activities will have to be curtailed by legislation resulting in a combination of taxation and rationing. All, rich and poor alike, must share the new low energy lifestyle.

Snowmobiles are just as bad. A typical 100-mile per hour sled gets 10 mpg. New 4-cycle machines are better but should be used only for absolute necessities. Why not go cross-country skiing instead? I'm certain there would be a concurrent improvement in overall health.

Postal Service, Catalogue mail order marketing, and other delivery service:

There is presently tremendous duplication and energy waste in the use of transportation energy. We can certainly do without unsolicited (junk) mail. We can use email, the web, and telephone for most communication. One or two package deliveries per week with substantial fuel surcharges to discourage all but the most essential shipments should keep our economy going just fine. Again, appropriate legislation will be required to effect these changes.

Space Travel and NASA:

As concluded before, only the pinnacle of the free energy age can support the effort of space exploration, and we are now passing that peak.

Why do we need further space exploration when our survival is at stake? Shouldn't we be focusing research and government subsidies to develop a fossil fuel free future?

---

2. Residential
(3.21 EBBO, 20% of energy consumption)

Residential energy use is almost as much as transportation. Of 3.21 EBBO per year, about one third is for heating and two thirds is for electricity. Using well know methods of conservation, turning the thermostats down, and being frugal with electricity, we should reduce this consumption by 50% in the next 10 years for a savings of 1.6 EBBO.

At the same ratio as present for heating and electricity, this new figure would give 1.1 EBBO for electricity and 0.5 EBBO for heating. If we assume 40 million homes, this would translate to 575 equivalent gallons of oil per year (most would be natural gas plus some wood) for heating, and for electricity, 34,000 kwh per year, or 2812 kwh/month.

This seems high for electricity for 40 million homes, but includes electric heat and substantial air-conditioning. We should reduce this by one half anyway. The above figures, at 50% present consumption, are still considerably more than the 200 kwh/month for electricity and 318 equivalent gallons of oil (from thermal solar) planned for the fossil fuel free residence (PR) in Chapter 4. The home heating consumption of 4800 kwh/yr ultimately planned from passive solar is equivalent to 215 equivalent gallons of oil burned at 50% efficiency. This energy would have to be supplemented by wood, coal, or oil and natural gas conserved from the 200 EBBO with our Five Percent per year reduction plan.

The above residential energy consumption includes hot water, which would be divided between the electrical and heating allotments depending on local price and availability.

The total residential saving at 50% of the 2001 consumption rate is 1.6 EBBO. Subtracting this from our reduced annual consumption of 13.2 EBBO (due to transportation savings) brings us down to 11.6 EBBO or about where we should be in 7 years (2010) on our Five Percent reduction plan.

Included in the above energy reduction in the residential area is any energy associated with extra living convenience. Only summertime alternative living arrangements are acceptable much like the summer retreat common in the 1800's. Today's larger homes will have to shrink into a warm living core area for the winter months.

To keep cool, we'll just have to rediscover the measures our great grand parents used. We may have to suffer a little and reschedule our day's and evening's activities. The people in the north will be better in the summer and the opposite is true for the southerners. In the winter we'll turn the thermostat down, wear more clothes, heat fewer rooms, be creative. Again, we'll probably be healthier for it.

The number one cropland in the USA with 32 million acres is the lawn. We will have to return this area to supplemental food production. The energy used to mow lawns would be far better used for growing food.

Everywhere in the rest of the world are small local gardens instead of lawns or wasted space. The return to home food production will make us appreciate how much we've come to depend on fossil fuels and energy intensive agribusiness. Remember, each adult requires about 500 pounds of high quality food (energy) per year. Our personal energy allowed us to procure that food input as hunter/gatherers and farmers as long as we did not deplete the resources. We are much healthier when we have a good personal balance between fuel intake and energy expense.

3. Commercial
(2.77 EBBO, 17% of Energy Consumption)

In 2001, commercial energy use was 0.67 EBBO for primary fossil fuel consumption and 2.1 EBBO for secondary electricity of which approximately 75% also comes from fossil fuels. The commercial sector is going to be more of a challenge for energy reduction because of its direct impact on jobs and economic activity. In the transportation and residential sectors, we only have to make personal changes in our lifestyle. Most energy reduction will not hurt as we take several steps backwards towards our great grandparent's quality of life. For our step by step descent down the Five Percent Plan and still keep our economy going, we will reduce the primary commercial fuel by only 25% and secondary commercial electricity by 50% (operating buildings less hours, turn down the heat, turn lights off, improve energy efficiency, use less space, etc.). This gives us savings of 1.2 EBBO (0.67 times 0.25 + 2.1 times 0.5 = 1.22 EBBO). Added to the previous savings this brings us down to 10.4 EBBO energy consumption per year. Now we are down to where we should be by the year 2012.

4. Industrial
(5.18 EBBO, 32% of Energy Consumption)

The final and largest sector of our energy intensive economy is industry which uses 5.18 EBBO per year at the present rate, proportioned as 3.43 EBBO as fossil fuels and 1.75 EBBO as electric power with approximately 75% also coming from fossil fuels. By reducing this consumption sector also by 50%, we save another 2.6 EBBO, which brings us down to 7.8 EBBO annual energy consumption. This is where we should be in the year 2018 on our Five Percent Plan and is about one half of our present (2003) energy consumption.

This leaves us another 22 years to eliminate another 2 EBBO and reach our final goal of 5.84 EBBO per year by the year 2040. This entire decrease in consumption is shown in the curve in Chapter 5. The actual numbers are summarized again in Appendix 4.

If we do not take control of our descent down the Five Percent per year energy plan, we will be nearly out of fuel by 2040. Energy costs will soon go out of control. World civilization as we know it will be doomed because we did not save enough fossil energy to reach a level of sustainability. We will not get another chance.

Both controlled and uncontrolled descents will incur significant fossil fuel reductions each successive year. The only difference is the Five Percent Plan occurs about 20 years earlier and leaves a very reasonable quality of life for our descendents. Leaving this critical issue another 20 years to the free market place and short-term interests will lead to world conflict, chaos, and misery as competing people fight for dwindling resources. We will then be effectively out of oil and natural gas with only dirty coal left, and can only hope to sustain a 3 EBBO per year level achieved with renewables, hydro, and nuclear, all of which depend on some fossil fuels for mining and manufacturing. Without the 200 EBBO of conserved fossil fuels we saved by starting immediately, 20 years sooner, civilization, as we know it will cease. We'll be out of gas.

Do we have the willpower to start saving now so our children will have a future? The next few years will tell. The 2004 election year will be critical for determining our direction.

Planning for the future sounds obvious and simple, but it may not happen because of denial, greed, and unwillingness of our leaders to comprehend and educate their constituents about the facts and hard choices. The impending crisis and demise of civilization will exceed all preceding wars and social upheaval in devastation, and we cannot win. Our only hope is for a majority of the voting public to urgently get behind this subject and encourage appropriate legislation which forces everyone to start now down the Five Percent Plan. We have no time to lose. Continuing to wobble along the top of Hubbert's Peak for the next few years will squander the most critical time at our present, prodigious, consumption rate.

If this scenario is overly pessimistic by a few years, hurray. It just means we have a little more time to get our act together and face the most important task ever to challenge humankind.

---

chapter 7

Related Issues, Summary and Call to Action

GEOPOLITICS

We now have a quantitative understanding of the short, fossil fuel energy age, of which only a small minority of the world's population is enjoying. Day by day world news takes on new meaning. A large part of the international chaos and turmoil has a major energy (or lack of energy) component. The industrialized world is intent on guarding its disproportionate share. Much of the Third World is already out of control because of overpopulation and dwindling or otherwise devastated natural resources made possible because of low cost energy and transportation. The 2003 issue of *State of the World*[1] identifies many energy related problems such as forest and soil depletion, mining devastation, and squalid slums adjacent to and living off the dregs of energy waste from major cities. Another comprehensive reference, which explores the relationship between resources and population is the book, *How Many People Can the Earth Support.*[2] It is especially discerning and prophetic to read the beginning of Chapter 16, "Case Study: Easter Island." The author quotes from his subject reference, "We consider that Easter Island was a microcosm which provides a model for the whole planet."[3]

In this case, a prolific isolated island of 166 square kilometers was completely denuded of trees in about a millennium. The civilization, which prospered and slowly grew to about 10,000 people, totally collapsed. Left behind were huge statues, up to 65 feet long standing and scattered as a testimonial to the short time energy surplus the natives enjoyed until increasing population and declining resources reached a collision point. It is interesting to note that the population crash occurred in only a couple of centuries compared to many more earlier years of good times. This completely isolated society lasted for many hundreds of years more than our fossil fuel, industrialized age can hope for.

While wandering around the web exploring references and links from www.hubbertpeak.com, I came across an interesting paper titled, *Busby Report, UK survival in the 21st Century*[4] and to quote the cover page:

> *The sun has set on the 20th century, when the "Black Gold" of oil provided the mobility for the creation of a global community. This report considers the measures to be taken to ensure the survival of the United Kingdom in a new century during which the world's oil will run out.*

Mr. Busby goes on to say,

> *We also have a huge task in preparing the British people for a change in lifestyle before a more unpleasant change is forced upon them by circumstances and to be able to re-direct capital and resources in a direction not currently taken, especially as it may contrast with that taken by the rest of Europe or of the world.*
>
> *As we face a future of global collapse in 25 to 50 years time, surely if the situation is properly explained and a sen-*

*sible and considered plan for survival through the 21st cen-
tury is promoted, the nation will rise to the task ... the time
table has started.*

*Whether the system dynamics forecasts are accurate is a
question merely of timing. If global economic collapse does not
occur around 2050, it will before the century is out. So national planning for survival runs only the risk of being a little premature.*

*We may have to unite in a united states of Europe to with-
stand the economic depredations of a USA wanting to secure
more than its share of dwindling energy and other resources.
Progress in alternative energy is currently more advanced in
Europe, in wind farms and with bio-diesel available at filling
stations. But if we put our own renewable resources in place in
the next crucial 10 years or so, while at the same time reorgan-
ize our economy to use a quarter of our current energy requirements, we will provide a model for a second industrial revolution in Europe and renew our world leadership in ideas.*

Busby then goes on to offer a plan for "national priorities" in
many areas and then offers two scenarios for "Britain in 2025."

*Here are two extreme scenarios-The first assumes that none
of the recommended actions have been taken, the second assumes
that all have been implemented.*

The first scenario goes on to describe a Europe in chaos combined with U.S. military reaction to maintain its threatened
lifestyle. The first scenario concludes with:

*However communications developed so that it is quite nor-
mal to see a horse and cart with the carter discussing customer
requirements with a mobile telephone.*

The second scenario goes on to describe a very acceptable economy and lifestyle with better health due to:

Fewer accidents on empty roads, participation in healthy sports and local activities. Drug-taking was finally brought under control not by policing but by the reduction in international traffic.

Unemployment is not the problem it might have foreseen to be as the lack of energy, to drive machinery, means that many functions have returned to manual labor.

... and so, on and on. Here you have an indication of recognition of the immediate pending crisis combined with a semblance of a plan and hope for a very acceptable future. Busby's plan is based on working down to 25% of the present U.K. energy consumption whereas the plan in Chapter 5 in this book is based on a U.S. reduction to a sustainable level that is closer to 40% of present consumption. This should be a much simpler task especially considering that we in the U.S. presently waste considerably more energy than the people in U.K. This is in large part because of $1.50/gallon instead of $4.50/gallon gasoline.

The message throughout the world is the U.S. is seen as the nation of bad energy guys, and inevitable future turmoil will further identify and isolate U.S. as the gluttons of world energy. Geopolitically, we need to reckon with this honest perception and use it to explain much of the evening news.

Rather than encumbering this short book with the complex synergism between geopolitics and energy, I'll leave the topic to many, more qualified sources. Numerous authors cited below, and in other chapters, devote considerable effort in the attempt to unravel the interaction of world politics and finite resources.[5,6,7,8,9] Obviously, these two subjects have been inextricably linked since the beginning of history. If we go back even farther, we can see the same phenomena taking place at all levels of biology and nature from squash bugs and potato beetles competing for plant space to mice overrunning a barn.

RELIGION

In these troubled times, the Islamic Middle East, which sits on top of most of the remaining world oil resources, is especially volatile. Millions of the younger generations are rendered irrelevant as more advanced societies move in, obviously interested only in the energy of their black gold. (Sounds a little bit like Spaniards and Aztecs). These indigenous people (rich and poor alike) turn to their strong religious fundamentalism to find answers, which in extreme cases clearly leads to terrorism. This is their only possible response to a vastly superior military presence. It is argued that oil is not the issue, but it certainly appears to be an underlying concern and common thread.

On a positive note, there is an inherently strong common bond between all religions and the environment. *The State of the World 2003*[1] concludes with an excellent chapter by Gary Gardner entitled: "Engaging Religion in the Quest for a Sustainable World." Mr. Gardner concludes:

... by combining their considerable skills and complimentary perspectives, environmentalists and religious people can help re-unite our civilizations head and heart. re-engaging religion in the quest for a new cosmology, a new world view for our time.

Another example is the conjunction of The National Council of Churches and the Sierra Club to fund expensive public ads to discourage drilling in ANWR.

Of 6 billion people in the world, Christianity (2 billion) and Islam (1.2 billion) are the largest. These religions, as well as the others like Hinduism (0.75 billion) and Buddhism (0.36 billion) teach respect and care for the natural world.

All successful indigenous societies had to have a strong environmental connection to be compatible with the laws of sustainability. If they didn't, it's Easter Island all over again.

91

Long-term civilizations usually survived until climate change, invasion from outside, or resource depletion upset their delicate energy balance with nature. Keep in mind, the great historic civilizations, like Mesopotamia, Egypt, Greece, and Rome lasted many more centuries than our present, two-century, fossil energy age. It appears, if outside forces threaten a society, strong religious ties work together to resist and protect that society's resources. But then, religion may not confront the most obvious cause of resource depletion, excessive population, which flourishes on bountiful resources and good times. Perhaps the classic confrontation between good and evil can be interpreted as a delicate interplay between consumption and supply. The periodic plagues of locusts or natural drought can be an interpretation of God's wraths for various sins. Maybe the Egyptians were closer to the truth in focusing on the sun god, Isus, as most important to life on earth with the sun as the source of life-giving energy.

If God had endowed us with a superior brain, he would expect us to use our skills to read the past, plan for the future, and do a far better job of resource utilization and conservation.

To quote the summarizing paragraph in the *State of the World 2003* reference,

> By combining their considerable skills and complimentary perspectives, environmental and religious people can help reunite our civilizations head and heart, re-engaging religion in the quest for a new cosmology, a new world view for our time. Cultural historian, Thomas Berry, calls this emerging perspective a New Story - the story of a people in an intimate and caring relationship with their planet, with their cosmos, and with each other.... It would be the vehicle to guide us to a socially just and environmentally sustainable future.[10]

I will conclude these thoughts about religion and sustainability by citing two other references. I, personally, don't believe in predestination, precognition, or causality (most engineers do not), but an interesting book came into my possession through a library book sale entitled, *Cracking the Apocalyptic Code*.[11] The authors describe the painstaking, numerical cracking of the apocalyptic code buried in the last book of the *Bible*, "The Book of Revelation," which "presages the end of humanity itself." This team of five experts worked laboriously together to expose the hidden prophecies and determine the date of Armageddon, the final battle between good and evil. The date they came up with is February 5, 2043, at midday. It's disturbing to note that most of the world oil experts are telling us that we have one trillion barrels left from the total original endowment of two trillion barrels at the beginning of the industrial age. We are using it at a rate of more than 28.5 billion barrels per year. Is it coincidence that this 35-year remainder to production ratio approximates the prophecy?

Secondly, I would like to call attention again to an excellent feature in *E-Magazine*.[12] The subheadings in this well researched article tell the story:

- "The Growing Religious Mission to Protect the Environment, Stewards of the Earth"

- "Science and Religion Meet"

- "Energy and Climate: Galvanizing Issues"

- "Active for Islam"

- "The Buddhist Way"

- "Hinduism's Green Tradition"

- "Jewish Reverence for Life"

- "Theological Dissent"

Only the last subheading, "Theological Dissent" offers contrasting opinions from the other side invoking "The Pastoral Division between God's Mission for Humankind: Stewardship or Dominion."

As with geopolitics, there is a strong connection between energy and religious interpretation for the rise and fall of mankind's fortunes. These interactions may not always be obvious, and sometimes they are contradictory. Using energy as a common theme may help clarify confusing and chronic questions all the way from the Bible to contemporary population issues.

SUMMARY AND CALL TO ACTION

So there you have it. An undeniable crisis is facing mankind. We can quibble about the details and exact timing, but there is no question that we've enjoyed a steep and pleasurable 100-year climb to a very precarious peak. The view is great, but we cannot linger a minute too long. We have to plan a careful descent while we still have fossil fuels left to descend our Five Percent per year transition to a low energy future.

Obviously, the greatest task is to reach and convince a majority of the voting American public that all is not well. This is extremely difficult considering the short-term happy face, feed back loop of a constituency, which elects representatives and leaders only to hear good news and avoid the bad. In an election campaign, bad news is a "no-no" except if the leadership can invent dragons, which make them look good while slaying them, an age-old ploy called job justification.

The real dragon is the coming energy crisis, but no one wants to hear the gloom and doom Cassandras.

We are like lemmings reputed to follow each other to their demise in the sea, a harsh form of population control. Short-term economic growth and prosperity takes precedence over long-term choices even if they are obviously contradictory. We will be no different than other animals if we don't consider the past, do the science and math, predict the future, and take appropriate, timely action. The timing and circumstances are critical and momentous. Consider the following 1989 quotation by William

D. Ruckelshaus, who was the administrator of the EPA under Nixon and Reagan.

Can we move nations and people in the direction of sustainability? Such a move would be a modification of society comparable in scale to only two other changes: The agricultural Revolution of the Late Neolithic and the Industrial Revolution of the past two centuries. These revolutions were gradual, spontaneous, and largely unconscious. This one will have to be a fully conscious operation, guided by the best foresight that science can provide.... If we actually do it, the undertaking will be absolutely unique in humanity's stay on the earth.[1]

If we collectively don't act soon, in the next few years, all is lost. Twenty more years of our unchecked, gross energy consumption will preclude any quality of life for our children. Look around and look to ourselves. Who are the takers?

How do we make something happen? This is the most important part of the book.

- **Project the Message in any form, in any way.** The importance of diminishing fossil fuel resources far exceeds any other subject except, possibly, personal health, to which it is indirectly related. Energy is certainly a part of food, shelter, work, recreation, and travel. Every part of your life should be reconsidered in terms of energy consumption. Raise a common voice. If individuals don't make it happen, all is lost.

- **Start to monitor world news** especially as related to energy. Read through the smoke and mirrors and put all related pieces of information into your own big picture. Check at least some of the websites and books referenced in this book. Cross-link to other sites.

- **Reconsider comprehensive planning**, short term and long range. All future plans related to energy will have to change. This especially includes family planning. Can the world provide for new mouths to feed when we won't have enough to go around? Will the coming quality of life be acceptable for us and our descendents? Look no further than sub-Saharan Africa, Ecuador, or India. Some parts of China are enjoying a temporary reprieve because of the influx of fossil energy and consumerism. Rural areas, however, are struggling with subsistence survival combined with dwindling resources. Unfortunately, even direct family planning will not quickly reduce the population component of the energy equation. It takes several generations for a decreased fertility ratio to take effect as the bulge of population numbers moves through the years towards old age. By buying time using the Five Percent per year reduction plan, we have the chance to eventually reduce population at a controlled rate proportional to decreased energy. Think of this fact; if, like energy consumption by 2150, we reduce population to about one fourth of the present 280 million, the per capita energy would be the same as today. By then, in 2150, hopefully we'll have worked out how to combine new technology with low energy lifestyles.

- **All community or national capital projects should be reconsidered**. Does it make sense to add a third lane to an interstate or expand an airport facility? We should be downsizing and questioning all planning, personal and public, in terms of future energy availability. We need to plan on a future with drastically reduced travel, heating, and air conditioning to name just a few of the many forms of plentiful energy to which we have become accustomed. Immediate investment should begin to quickly expand the manufacture of photovoltaic cell and wind generating equipment. Plans should be made to recycle large vehicles into 60 mpg diesel or hybrid cars. These will be the last generation of personal vehicles before fully electric cars become the only alternative to the bicycle or walking. The work force should be directed towards a low energy future instead of perpetuating the past.

As this book is being finalized, the Ford Motor Company is celebrating its 100th anniversary. (There's that 100-year time span again.) So what are they doing? They're introducing a new, bigger and better, F150 pickup truck for the public, and at the same time planting grass on their new factory roofs to appease the environmentalists.

- **Personal Changes.** Make plans now to move towards energy efficiency, reduced travel, smaller insulated homes, solar and wind generation, and reduced consumerism. This especially should exclude the marketing and advertising of energy intensive products. Of course, there'll be immediate changes required by everyone, but it is our only chance. Don't believe that things are happening automatically. Inertia continues on the easiest path. You've heard much of this before, yet we're still moving steadily in the wrong direction.

We must gain a majority in our democracy so the required action becomes law for all. The future lies with with legislation directed towards food, shelter, warmth, reduced population, and any other activities that use only a minimum of energy.

THIS BOOK

The purpose of writing this book is to reach the public on the very important subject of fossil energy depletion. Hopefully I've made the reader aware of the comprehensive story of energy and fossil fuels. The expense for initial publishing is coming from my pocket, my children's inheritance, for obvious reasons. It is their only chance for a future. This book is copyrighted and may be reproduced except for resale or profit and with proper credit. The intent is for anyone to use the message, as is, or in any way or form to reach exponential numbers of readers as quickly as possible. Any number of additional complete books can be purchased individually for $10.00 each, which covers further printing, handling, and shipping costs. Volume pricing is approximately 50% as much depending on quantity. For further information write to Howe Engineering Company, P.O. Box 2038, Norway, ME 04268 or contact the publisher at www.mcintirepublishing.com.

There is no glory being the harbinger of bad news. There is nothing new or unique in this book. It is only a compilation of existing facts, science, math, and logic.

All I've attempted to do is to distill and simplify the huge subject of energy, especially in the finite fossil fuel form, and how it will affect civilization as we know it. I've tried to offer an engineer's vision of a downstream, low energy, but still industrialized lifestyle. My career work has been in new product development. As related to energy, I have manufactured and marketed bicycle powered generators and grain threshers. It was this work, that first convinced me how feeble the human body is for converting food energy to useful work. I will continue, in every way possible, to further study, monitor, and project the message of declining fossil fuels. I am also constructing a prototype of a combination electric transportation vehicle and small farm tractor or EUV, (see Chapter 4 and the back cover). A machine like this may realistically be the only hope for an industrialized, post-fossil fuel future.

My EUV will be powered from our residential photovoltaic system. I hope to prove (as many others have already) that a reduced energy lifestyle will be very acceptable and more rewarding than the forced consumerism treadmill that now controls us.

The future of the civilized world (hopefully led by the U.S.) depends on acceptance of and action taken from this and many similar messages. I hope I'm around long enough to see a direction change before it's too late. Don't be deluded into thinking that the problem is non-existent or is being overstated. The problem is our gross consumption of energy. We are the problem, and if we don't change there is no hope.

In conclusion, I offer a quotation from a lecture series titled, "Of Men and Galaxies" given 39 years ago, in 1964, at the University of Washington by cosmologist, Sir Fred Hoyle:

> *It is often said that, if the human species fails to make a go of it here on earth, some other species will take over the running. In the sense of developing high intelligence this is not correct. We have, or soon will have, exhausted the necessary physical prerequisites so far as this planet is concerned. With coal gone, oil gone, high-grade metallic ores gone, no species however competent can make the long climb from primitive conditions to high-level technology. This is a one shot affair. If we fail, this planetary system fails so far as intelligence is concerned. The same will be true of other planetary systems. On each of them there will be one chance, and one chance only.*

This is exactly the prediction proposed in the *Olduvai Theory* discussed at the end of Chapter 4.[14]

To repeat an earlier statement, civilization will not survive unless individuals make it happen. Get involved. Pass it on. It is especially important, considering that time is of the essence, that we reach influential leaders or media that can, in turn, quickly reach a much broader audience. We cannot give up, no matter how futile our efforts may at first appear.

footnotes

Chapter 1

[1] Seidel, P., *Invisible Walls: Why We Ignore the Damage We Inflict on the Planet ... and Ourselves*, (New York: Prometheus Books, 1998).
[2] Deffeyes, K., *Hubbert's Peak: the impending world oil shortage*, (Princeton, NJ: Princeton University Press, 2001).

Chapter 2

[1] Smil, V., *Energies*, (Massachusetts: MIT Press, 1999).
[2] www.world-nuclear.org.
[3] Rifkin, J., *The Hydrogen Economy*, (New York: Parcher/Putnam, 2002).
[4] Hoffman, Peter, *Tomorrow's Energy*, (Massachusetts: MIT Press, 2002).
[5] Lovins, A., various papers on hydrogen energy available from R.M.I. (The Rocky Mountain Institute).
[6] Bockris, J., *Energy, The Solar-Hydrogen Alternative*, (New York: John Wiley & Sons, 1975).
[7] www.hydrogenus.com.
[8] www.hydrogennow.org.
[9] www.copvia.com see articles on hydrogen as well as many more refering to peak oil.

Chapter 3 *Copvc1A*

[1] Deffeyes, K., *Hubbert's Peak* (New Jersey: Princeton University Press, 2001).
[2] Campbell, C.J., *The Essence of Oil &Gas Depletion* (Multi-Science Publishing Company and Petroconsultants, 2003).
[3] www.eia.doe.gov, (Energy Information Agency), 2001, 2002, 2003.
[4] Stobaugh, R., Yergin, D., Editors, *Energy Future*: A Report of the Energy Project at the Harvard Business School (New York: Ballantine Books, 1979).
[5] Yergin, D., *The Prize* (New York: Free Press, 1991).
[6] Meadows, D.H. and D.L., *Beyond the Limits, Confronting Global Collapse, Envisioning a Sustainable Future* (Vermont: Chelsea Green Publishing, 1992).
[7] Passerini, E., *The Curve of the Future* (Alabama: The Environmental Action Clearing House, 1991).
[8] Rifkin, J., *The Hydrogen Economy* (New York: Tarcher/Putnam, 2002), Chapter 2.
[9] Behr, P., "Of Drills and Energy Bills," *The Washington Post*, 26 May - 1 June 2003, p. 20.
[10] Bradsher, K., *High and Mighty* (New York: Public Affairs, 2002
[11] www.bts.gov (Bureau of Transportation Statistics).

[12] Gore, A., *The Earth in Balance* (New York: Houghton Mifflin, 1992), p. 173.
[13] www.worldwatch.com
[14] www.cees.com, or www.bu.edu/cees
[15] www.nrel.gov

Chapter 4

[1] Scheer, Dr. H., *The Solar Economy* (London: Earthscan Publications, 2002).
[2] Duncan, R.C., *The Olduvai theory* (Institute on Energy and Man, 1996) www.greatchange.org/othervoices.
[3] Pfeiffer, Dale Allen, *From the Wilderness*, newsletters. Oct., Nov., Dec. 2003 www.copvia.com.

Chapter 5 *Copvcia*

[1] Klare, Michael, *Resource Wars: The New Landscape of Global Conflict* (New York: Henry Holt and Co., 2001).
[2] Kaplan. Robert D., *The Coming Anarchy: Shattering the Dreams of the Post Cold War* (New York: Random House, 2000).
[3] Homer-Dixen, Thomas, *Environment, Scarcity, and Violence* (New Jersey: Princeton University Press, 1999).
[4] Duncan, R.C., *The Olduvai Theory* (Institute on Energy and Man, 1996). (www.greatchange.org/othervoices).
[5] Price, David R., (www.greatchange.org)
[6] Heinberg, R.,*The Party's Over: Oil, War, and the Fate of Industrialized Societies* (B.C. Canada: New Society Publishers, 2003). (www.newsociety.com)
[7] Thompson, B., ().
[8] Korpela, S., (www.greatchange.org/othervoices).
[9] Grover, J. et al., *Beyond Oil: the Threat to Food and Fuel in the Coming Decades* (Colorado: University Press of Colorado, 1991).
[10] www.apolloalliance.org

Chapter 6

[1] The World Watch Institute, *State of the World 2003*, (New York: W.W. Norton, 2003)
[2] Campbell, C.J., "The Imminent Peak of World Oil Production," presentation to the House of Commons, 7 July 1999
[3] Abraham, Spencer (U.S. Energy Secretary) remarks to the Detroit Economic Club, 7 February 2003 www.eere.energy.gov.
[4] EIA, *Energy Review*, (1991 to 2001), fig.1.3.
[5] Heinberg, Richard, *The Party's Over: Oil, War, and the Fate of Industrial Societies*, (New Society Publishers, 2003).

Chapter 7

[1] World Watch Institute,*State of the World 2003*, (W.W. Norton), (www.worldwatch.com).
[2] Cohen, Joel E., *How Many People Can the Earth Support*, (W.W. Norton, 1995).
[3] Bahn, Paul G., and Flenley, John, *Easter Island, Earth Island*, (New York: Thames and Hudson, 1992).

[4] www.afteroil.co.uk

[5] Heinberg, Richard. *The Party's Over*,(B,C. Canada: New Society Publications, 2003), (www.newsociety.com).

[6] Yergin, D., *The Prize, The Epic Quest for Oil, Money, and Power*, (New York: Free Press, 1991).

[7] Rifkin, J. *The Hydrogen Economy*, (New York: Tarcher Putnam, 2002).

[8] Meadows, Dennis and Donella Meadows, *Beyond the Limits*, (Vermont: Chelsea Green Publishing, 1992).

[9] Brown, A., *Oil, God and Gold: The Story of Aramco and Saudi Kings*, (New York: Houghton Mifflin, 1999).

[10] Swimme, T., and Berry, *The Universe Story*, (New York: Harper Collins, 1992).

[11] Bodson, G., *Cracking the Apocalyptic Code*, (Boston: Element Books, 2000).

[12] *E-Magazine*, Volume XIII, No. 6, Nov/Dec 2002.

[13] Ruckelshaus, W.D., *Scientific American*, "Toward a Sustainable World," September 1989.

[14] www.greatchange.org/othervoices

appendix 1

Solar Energy Calculation

40 million homes each with a 2 to 4 peak kilowatt photovoltaic system (depending on location) could provide an average of 400 kwh/m or 4800 kwh/yr. (6.6 hrs. to 3.3 hrs./day average sunlight):

$$40 \times 10^6 \times 4800 \text{ kwh/yr/home} \times 3{,}412 \text{ BTU/kwh}$$
$$= 655 \times 10^{12} \text{ BTU}$$

$$655 \times 10^{12} \text{ BTU} \times 0.159 \text{ EBBO}/10^{15} \text{ BTU}/.35 \text{ efficiency}$$
$$= 0.3 \text{ EBBO}$$

(This compares to the 2001 solar U.S. photovoltaic production of 0.01 EBBO)

Add residential non-photovoltaic (passive and active) solar for hot water and domestic heating equal to the photovoltaic component:

$$0.3 \text{ EBBO} + 0.3 \text{ EBBO} = 0.6 \text{ EBBO}$$

Photovoltaic output from centralized (CDF) power plants would equal the total solar output from residential (PR) distributed sources. The total solar output (photovoltaic and non-photovoltaic) from all sources would be:

$$0.6 \text{ EBBO} + 0.6 \text{ EBBO} = 1.2 \text{ EBBO}$$

In other words, it would take 1.2 EBBO of fossil fuel input from power plants to provide the direct solar energy output expected from our model.

To summarize the proposed annual U.S. photovoltaic electricity production by 2050:

$$0.3 \text{ EBBO (PR)} + 0.6 \text{ EBBO (CDF)} = 0.9 \text{ EBBO}$$

This is the equivalent fossil fuel that would be required at 35% efficiency to produce the end use (secondary) annual electricity as follows:

$$192 \times 10^9 \text{ kwh (PR)} + 384 \times 10^9 \text{ kwh (CDF)}$$
$$= 576,000 \times 10^6 \text{ kwh}$$

It will be an incredibly daunting task to reach this solar photovoltaic output by 2050. At an average insolation of 150 hours/month or 1800 hours/year, the total installed photovoltaic production capacity in U.S. alone would have to be

$$576,000 \times 10^6 \text{ kwh/yr. divided by 1800 hrs./yr.}$$
$$= 320,000 \text{ mw}$$

For the next 45 years until 2050, this much capacity would require an average PV production and installation of 7,111 mw each year. As of 2002, the PV cell/module production in U.S. was 120 mw and in the total world it was 562 mw[1]. This means we must increase U.S. PV production sixty times (!!) in order to move to a true solar powered economy. Obviously, we need to get started as soon as possible. If we wait for the market forces and prices of declining fossil fuels to motivate us, it will be too late.

Footnotes:

[1] PV News, Vol. 22, No. 3, March 2003.

appendix 2

Human Energy Requirements

We will start with 2000 kilocalorie (C) average energy intake required daily by 200 million adults. This equates to an annual energy requirement as follows:

$$2000C \times 200 \times 10^6 \times 365 \times 3.968 \text{ BTU/C}$$
$$\times 0.159 \text{ EBBO}/10^{15} \text{ BTU} = 0.092 \text{ EBBO}$$

If we add another 90 million children each requiring 1000 kilocalories per day, we find a total U.S. energy intake for food of 0.113 EBBO.

If we assume an approximate factor of 10 to find the energy required to bring this food to our table, we end up with about 1 EBBO per year just to feed our present population. This tenfold increase includes the energy for crop tillage, planting, fertilizer, harvesting, processing, waste, packaging, presentation, and marketing.

There is much confusion and complexity regarding this subject; for instance, it has been estimated that the energy content required to feed animals to be subsequently used for human consumption is ten times the energy used if the plant food went directly to human use. The intent in this (Appendix 2) discussion is only to show the order of energy magnitude just to fuel our most important machines, our bodies.

appendix 3

Planned 50% Reduction in Residential Energy Use

We will start with the EIA total for the residential sector in 2001 of 20.2 x 10^{15} BTU or 3.21 EBBO. Of this total 6.9 x 10^{15} BTU pr 1.1 EBBO is primary consumption of fuel for heating and the balance of 2.1 EBBO is secondary energy used as electricity.

The heating component of 1.1 EBBO is equivalent to:

$$1.1 \text{ EBBO x 42 gal/barrel} = 46.2 \times 10^9 \text{ gal}$$

If we assume 40 million homes, this works out to 1,150 gal. oil (or equivalent natural gas) per home. Multiplying this by one half means we will still have 575 gal. per year for heating. Anywhere else in the world, this much energy for heating would be positively opulent. With the proposed 5% reduction plan, even this home heating energy will have to be further reduced to eventually approach only what is available from non-photovoltaic solar. In Chapter 4, a typical solar home is described with 400 kwh per month of electricity component and an equal amount of solar heating. On a yearly basis the non-photovoltaic would be:

$$4800 \text{ kwh/yr. x 3412 BTU/kwh x 1 gal./52,000 BTU}$$

(equivalent oil is assumed at 35% efficiency or 0.35 times 150,000 BTU/gal.)

This equals 314 gal. per home with no fossil fuels used ... down to about 55% of our proposed interim level of 575 gal. per year.

The purpose of this exercise is to show the declining levels of home heating energy (including some hot water) we will have to go through to reach a sustainable civilization.

The electrical component of 2.1 EBBO is equivalent to:

$$\text{2.1 EBBO}/0.159 = 0.35 \text{ EFF.} \times 13.21 \times 10^{15} \text{ BTU}$$
$$/3{,}412 \text{ BTU/kwh}$$

This equates to 1.35×10^{12} kwh. If this much energy is provided to 40 million homes it would equal 2,812 kwh/month. This seems high for residential usage but includes considerable electric heating, air conditioning and apartments.

If we reduce this by 50% per our Five Percent Plan it still leaves us with 1,406 kwh/month. Far more than the 400 kwh/month estimated for both residential electricity and personal transportation in Chapter 4. There is considerable room here to allow for additional reductions in residential electricity consumption and reach our goal of 5.85 EBBO by the year 2050.

appendix 4

The Five Percent Plan:

A TIME LINE FOR A CONTROLLED DESCENT AND SYSTEMATIC ENERGY REDUCTION TO REACH A LOW ENERGY FUTURE

The following summary table shows the total U.S. energy consumption goal for each successive year at a Five Percent annual reduction. These goals are compared to actual reduction that could be achieved as proposed in Chapter 6.

Year	Five Percent Goal	Actual "Reductions Achieved Per Chapter 6
2004	16	Start Five Percent Plan on Jan 1, 2005 at 2003 U.S. consumption level of 16 EBBO
2005	15.2	Large cars and trucks @ 18 mpg to 35 mpg cars. Annual savings = 0.86 EBBO. New level = 15.14 EBBO
2006	14.4	Reduce personal travel by 50%. Annual savings = 0.86 EBBO New level = 14.28 EBBO

(continued on next page)

Year	Five Percent Goal	Actual Reductions Achieved Per Chapter 6
2007	13.72	Switch from 35 mpg to 60 mpg vehicles. Annual savings = 0.36 EBBO New level = 13.92 EBBO
2008	13.03	Curtail diesel fuel and airplane travel by 50%. Annual savings = 0.77 EBBO New level = 13.15 EBBO
2009 2010	12.38 11.76	Reduce residential energy consumption by 50%. Annual savings in electricity = 1.1 EBBO. Annual savings in primary fuel = 0.5 EBBO. Total annual savings = 1.6 EBBO. New level = 11.55 EBBO
2011 2012	11.17 10.61	Reduce commercial consumption by 25% of primary fuel and 50% of electricity. Total annual savings = 1.2 EBBO. New level = 10.35 EBBO
2013 2014 2015 2016 2017 2018	10.08 9.58 9.10 8.65 8.21 7.80	Reduce industrial consumption by 50%. Annual savings = 2.6 EBBO. New level = 7.75 EBBO or where we should be by 2018. This gives us another 22 years to reach our sustainable level goal of 5.85 by the year 2040. Obviously these reductions in each of four consumption sectors will not be made in series but should occur in parallel to reach each annual Five Percent reduction goal.
2019 Jump to 2040	7.41 5.85	Reduce all consumption another two EBBO between 2018 and 2040 as we move toward a totally renewable energy economy while simultaneously conserving 200 EBBO of fossil fuels.

appendix 5

Summary of Total World Regular Oil Production:

PAST AND FUTURE PREDICTED FOR ALL COUNTIES RANKED BY ORIGINAL ENDOWMENT EXCLUDING OIL FROM COAL, SHALE, BITUMIN, HEAVY, DEEPWATER, POLAR, AND PLANT NGL (NATURAL GAS LIQUIDS).

All figures in Gb (Giga barrels), same as billion of barrels or EBBO as of 2002.

	Country	Past Production	Future Known and New	Total Original Endowment	Percent depleted
1	Saudi Arabia	94	206	300	31
2	Russia	121	79	200	61
3	U.S.	171	21	191	90
4	Iraq	27	108	135	20
5	Iran	54	76	130	42
6	Venezuela	46	49	95	48
7	Kuwait	31	59	90	34
8	Abu Dhabi	18	60	78	23
9	China	27	30	57	47
10	Libya	23	32	55	42
11	Nigeria	22	33	55	40
12	Mexico	30	25	55	55
13	Kazakhstan	6	34	40	15
14	Norway	16	17	33	48
15	U.K.	20	12	32	63
16	Indonesia	20	11	31	65
17	Algeria	12	16	28	43
18	Canada	19	6	25	76
19	Azerbaijan	8	15	23	35
20	N. Zone	7	9	16	44
21	Oman	7	8	15	47
22	Qatar	7	6	13	54
23	Egypt	9	4	13	69
24	India	6	6	12	50
25	Argentina	8	4	12	67
26–64	Next 38 countries combined	87	78	166	52
	World Total	896	1004	1900	47

Per EIA statistics, at the 2002 rate of 78 million barrels per day (28.47 EBBO annually), total depletion would occur 35 years after 2002. By 2004 this reduces to approximately 33 years. Per EIA projections, if consumption increased to 118 million barrels per day (42 EBBO) by 2025, world consumption between 2002 and 2025 would average 35 EBBO annually for 23 years for a total of 805 EBBO. By 2025 we will have used 80% of our remaining known and new reserves of 1004 EBBO.

The message is clear. In the past 150 years, we have completed the first one half of the age of oil. At the present rate of consumption, we will compress the second half into less than 40 years. At the EIA forecasted increase rate, we will be empty in 28 years.

The above table was reproduced by permission from page 237 of *The Essence of Oil and Gas Depletion* by C. J. Campbell, published in 2003 by Multi-Science Publishing Co., Essex, England. Tel: (01277)224632.